INTEGRATING LITERACY AND MATH

TOOLS FOR TEACHING LITERACY

Donna Ogle and Camille Blachowicz, Series Editors

This highly practical series includes two kinds of books: (1) grade-specific titles for first-time teachers or those teaching a particular grade for the first time; (2) books on key literacy topics that cut across all grades, such as integrating literacy with technology and science, teaching literacy through the arts, and fluency. Written by outstanding educators who know what works based on extensive classroom experience, each research-based volume features hands-on activities, reproducibles, and best practices for promoting student achievement. These books are suitable as texts for undergraduate- or graduate-level courses; preservice teachers will find them informative and accessible.

INTEGRATING LITERACY AND MATH

STRATEGIES FOR K–6 TEACHERS

Ellen Fogelberg
Carole Skalinder
Patti Satz
Barbara Hiller
Lisa Bernstein
Sandra Vitantonio

Series Editors' Note by Donna Ogle and Camille Blachowicz

THE GUILFORD PRESS
New York   London

© 2008 The Guilford Press
A Division of Guilford Publications, Inc.
72 Spring Street, New York, NY 10012
www.guilford.com

Printed in the United States of America

This book is printed on acid-free paper.

Last digit is print number: 9 8 7 6 5 4 3 2 1

Library of Congress Cataloging-in-Publication Data

Integrating literacy and math : strategies for K–6 teachers / Ellen Fogelberg ...
[et al.].
      p. cm. — (Tools for teaching literacy)
   Includes bibliographical references and index.
   ISBN 978-1-59385-718-9 (pbk.: alk. paper) — ISBN 978-1-59385-719-6
(hardcover: alk. paper)
   1. Mathematics—Study and teaching (Elementary) 2. Language arts—
Correlation with content subjects. I. Fogelberg, Ellen.
   QA135.6.I58 2008
   372.7—dc22
                                                        2008006885

ABOUT THE AUTHORS

Ellen Fogelberg, MST, CAS, has been a classroom teacher, reading specialist, and staff developer. She is currently the Literacy Director for the Evanston/Skokie School District and an adjunct professor at National-Louis University, teaching in the graduate program for Reading. Ms. Fogelberg has presented at state and national conferences and continues to provide workshops for teachers. She received the Reading Educator of the Year award in 2007 from the Illinois Reading Council.

Carole Skalinder, MST, has taught in public and private schools for over 30 years. While teaching third grade in Evanston, Illinois, for the last 14 years, she has also worked as a part-time math coach for her school district. She provides professional development in math curriculum and instruction for many groups of practicing and beginning teachers. Ms. Skalinder collaborated with Donna Ogle and other educators to develop an integrated science and literacy curriculum and has presented the resulting student work at local and national conferences. She participated in the revision of a major standards-based math curriculum.

Patti Satz, MEd, has been teaching first and second grade for 32 years in Evanston School District 65. She has been a math curriculum and instruction coach for 3 years and has been a consultant for a major standards-based math curriculum revision. She has also been a math curriculum presenter at numerous professional workshops. Ms. Satz has trained new teachers in her district in math instruction for many years, and was the recipient of the 2002 Excellence in Mentoring Award from Northwestern University and the Evanston Chamber of Commerce.

Barbara Hiller, MS, is presently serving as a principal coach for the Consortium for Educational Change in Illinois. A former middle school mathematics teacher in Athens, Greece, and Evanston, Illinois, Ms. Hiller has also served as a math curriculum coordinator, middle school principal, and consultant to the University of

Chicago Everyday Mathematics development project. As a Peace Corps volunteer in the early years of the program, she taught mathematics at the Philippine Normal College, training new teachers and providing staff development throughout the country. Ms. Hiller retired as the Assistant Superintendent for Curriculum and Instruction in the Evanston/Skokie School District in Illinois.

Lisa Bernstein, MEd, currently teaches third grade in the Evanston/Skokie public schools in Illinois. As a proponent of the improvement of elementary math education, she works with various programs, including Northwestern University's Project EXCITE and the University of Chicago's Center for Elementary Mathematics and Science Education, and presents math workshops for teachers throughout Illinois.

Sandra Vitantonio, MEd, is an educator in Evanston, Illinois, and was a classroom teacher for 34 years. During this time, she received an award from the Illinois State Board of Education as part of its Those Who Excel Awards Program, and was nominated for the Kohl Teaching Award by her school district. She also worked at the University of Chicago on the Everyday Mathematics curriculum project. She retired from teaching in 2005 and is currently working as a mentor coach for new teachers in Evanston/Skokie District 65.

SERIES EDITORS' NOTE

This is an exciting time to be involved in literacy education. Across the United States, thoughtful practitioners and teacher educators are developing and fine-tuning their instructional practices to maximize learning opportunities for children. These cutting-edge practices deserve to be shared more broadly. Because of these changes, we have become aware of the need for a series of books for thoughtful practitioners who want a practical, research-based overview of current topics in literacy instruction. We also collaborate with staff developers and study group directors who want effective inservice materials that they can use with professionals and colleagues at many different levels that provide specific insights about literacy instruction. Thus the Tools for Teaching Literacy series was created.

This series is distinguished by having each volume written by outstanding educators who are noted for their knowledge and contributions to research, theory, and best practices in literacy education. They are also well-known staff developers who spend time in real classrooms working alongside teachers applying these insights. We think the series authors are unparalleled in these qualifications.

In this important addition to our collection, a team of reflective curriculum leaders and teachers share the results of their several-year collaboration creating effective math instruction for a diverse population of students. Their practical and carefully worked out instructional routines are based on listening to and assessing students' learning needs. They have identified specific ways that math lessons pose literacy challenges to their students and now, in this volume, share the ways they have found to provide literacy instruction that is needed in math and to use math content in literacy development. An outstanding feature is the attention the authors give to developing students' use of oral language for learning.

DONNA OGLE
CAMILLE BLACHOWICZ

PREFACE

The study of mathematics is much more than the solving of an arithmetic problem or the solving of a word problem using a recently taught algorithm. Expectations for our students have changed, necessitating a change in our instructional role as "teacher." We still expect our students to know their facts, to learn algorithms, and to solve problems, but we can no longer teach these skills through repeated drill and practice without conceptual understanding.

As you look into our classrooms, you see a very different structure, not only physically but also in the teacher-to-student and student-to-student relationships. You hear mathematical conversations, see students working with the tools of mathematics, and doing mathematical writing individually, with partners, or in small groups. Our students are reading, talking, and writing in order to make sense of mathematical questions and to develop strategies for solving these questions or problems.

As teachers, we encourage all students to listen, to question, to discuss their observations, and to share their reasoning. It is important for students to clarify their thinking as they make sense of mathematical concepts and not simply to be right or wrong. Posing open-ended questions allows students to give a variety of responses, describe patterns, make predictions, and question their own understandings in a supportive classroom. We are teaching our students to become reflective learners by encouraging them to explore the ideas of peers, the teacher, and themselves.

We are a group of educators who have worked together over the last several years to improve our instruction and to create classrooms where the day makes sense to us and our students. This happens because we have found ways to connect the learning throughout the day. We have integrated our instruction in important ways and share how we did so in this book. The majority of the student examples come from the students in Carole Skalinder's and Patti Satz's classrooms. Barbara Hiller and Ellen Fogelberg, from the Evanston District 65 Curriculum Department, have worked with Carole and Patti for several years as staff developers and colleagues. Many of the ideas and instructional practices presented here are the result of their collaboration. Sandra Vitantonio and Lisa Bernstein have contributed additional student work and supported the development of this project. Although most of our examples come from grades 2, 3, and 5, we believe that the work can be used in grades 1–6. Kindergarten teachers in our district integrate math and literacy instruction through calendar activities and in the designated math and literacy blocks.

Chapter 1 describes teachers' work in the classroom, using talking, reading, and writing skills to help students better understand and use mathematics. The reader will find suggestions for setting up a language-rich math classroom as well as an overview of the strategies for integrating math and literacy learning that is developed in detail in the chapters that follow.

In Chapter 2, we describe what is meant by math talk and give examples that will start children talking about mathematics, taking risks, and making assertions and conjectures. The reader will find examples of anchor charts for partner reading and problem solving along with suggestions for creating new anchor charts.

How do we get started helping our students get better at math talk? Chapter 3 focuses on planning for mathematical conversations—both student-led and whole-group discussions. The basis for successful inquiry is making students comfortable in expressing and explaining their strategies as they learn to solve problems and come to a consensus.

Math texts present challenging reading to many of our students. In Chapter 4, we offer strategies for addressing vocabulary, concepts, and text structure. A discussion of grouping strategies—whole group, small group, partner reading, and individual work—is an important part of this chapter.

Chapter 5 continues the conversation of actively reading math texts using the same cognitive strategies used when reading in other content areas. The reader will find examples of lessons, as well as strategies and instructional routines that help students become engaged while reading the text.

Chapter 6 provides a discussion of lessons that are designed to increase students' ability to use the language of mathematics to solve problems and make sense of the world. The reader will find a range of instructional strategies for teaching mathematical terms and concepts.

Chapter 7 looks at mathematical writing as a tool that provides the teacher with a way to look at individual student strategies and understandings, as well as a way for students to reflect and revise their own thinking. Journal writing, mathematical arguments, writing prompts, and creative writing are described.

Assessment, as a guide to instruction, is described in Chapter 8. Formal and informal observations, pretests, end-of-unit tests, and specific literacy products, such as talking, writing, and responding to reading, are included in the assessments used to measure progress. The reader will find different ways to assess students' understanding through their use of language and their ability to articulate their understanding.

We continue to collaborate with each other and with the rest of the teachers in the district. This is our life's work. Our students continue to inspire and teach us every day. We hope readers find ideas and examples to support efforts at integration.

We would be remiss if we didn't acknowledge others who helped us put this book together. We thank our students and their families and the many teachers who have helped shape our thinking and work. A special thanks to Rosalie Ziomek, who drew the figures for the bookmark described in Chapter 5. Finally, we thank our families; the series editors, Donna Ogle and Camille Blachowicz; and the editors at The Guilford Press for their patience and support during the development of this project.

CONTENTS

INTEGRATING LITERACY AND MATH

CHAPTER 1

WHAT IS MATH–LITERACY INTEGRATION?

On the way to the gym, the class is not quiet in the hallway. They have just come from a math lesson, and are still talking about equivalent fractions. " . . . twelve-eighteenths; fourteen twenty-oneths [sic]; sixteen twenty-fourths. Do you get the pattern? Do you get it now? The numerators go up by twos. The denominators go up by threes. Wow! It's so cool!"

The way we teach math now is different from the way we were taught. Math was quite separate from reading, and in math we remember solving pages of problems. As the dispenser of knowledge, the teacher presented the math concept of the day. There was the occasional question by a student who wasn't sure what page we were on, but otherwise there was little dialogue between the teacher and the students and no math conversation among the students. The teacher explained how the problem should be solved, and that was it. There were no alternate approaches to solving the problem. The homework was assigned and the routine continued day after day, year after year.

Many teachers, like their students, still think of math as a totally separate subject from language arts. They may not see the connections to what students are learning during reading and writing instruction. Or if they do, they may not know how to make those math–literacy connections explicit or use them effectively. Helping teachers to see these links and making them work in their classrooms is the purpose of this book.

Math class can be a very exciting, vibrant part of the day. The teacher challenges students and they can challenge each other about mathematical concepts. When the teacher says, "Tell me what you think about that," or "What do you not understand?" students begin to comment and ask questions. They reflect on their thinking processes, hear each other, and build on each other's ideas. These budding mathematicians enter into passionate discussions with a point of view. Hearing

1

other arguments, they rethink their ideas and strengthen their understandings. All of this becomes possible when current standards for school mathematics are implemented and integrated with literacy skills. As teachers, we have become more intentional about using reading, writing, and talking in math class and, as a result, we see increased understanding of math concepts and problem solving. And, by bringing math vocabulary, math trade books, and some math writing into our language arts block, we've helped students make connections across subject areas. Our students are figuring out that the thinking and learning they do in all subject areas is related.

With the recent increase in availability of math trade books, teachers have another category of informational texts to use for shared, guided, and independent reading. Teaching for understanding is easier with these additional print resources and they contribute to making the mathematics come alive. These visually appealing books illustrate a context for the mathematical concepts under study and provide models for students to use in problem solving and written explanations for solutions. Pape (2004), writing in the *Journal for Research in Mathematics Education* suggests that "problem solvers' use of context and their ability to provide explanations and justifications for their problem-solving steps are critical to constructing accurate mental models for mathematical word problems" (p. 212).

As defined in another book in this series, *Integrating Instruction: Literacy and Science*, language literacy means "the ability to use reading and writing, speaking and listening sufficiently well to engage in thinking and to communicate ideas. . . . Foundational to all language acquisition is that students develop the ability to think" (McKee & Ogle, 2005, p. 2). Hyde (2006) uses the term "braiding" to demonstrate how thinking, language, and mathematics come together to help students become better problem-solvers. The thinking strategies are the same cognitive strategies used for engaging with and understanding any new learning. Students rely on language skills to read, write, talk, and represent their mathematical thinking and problem solving. In this book, we provide many examples of how we merge, or braid, the thinking and language strategies throughout our mathematics instruction.

CURRENT STANDARDS FOR TEACHING MATHEMATICS

As elementary school teachers, we are responsible for providing students with the knowledge and strategies necessary for understanding and using mathematics. The *Principles and Standards for School Mathematics* (National Council of Teachers of Mathematics [NCTM], 2000) define the skills and strategies that students should know and be able to use effectively (see Appendix A). According to a recent article in *Education Update* (Saul, 2006, p. 1), the standards "emphasize the following practices as important to providing an effective math curriculum":

> helping young students learn to "think algebraically," leading to greater achievement in high school;

> emphasizing problem solving as early as kindergarten, so students learn to pull problems apart and identify their essence;

> developing deep and meaningful understanding of mathematics by helping students talk and write about the significance of their math learning.

Thinking Algebraically

In the book *Algebra for Everyone,* Howden (1990, p. 21) states, "Preparation for success in algebra includes much more than computational proficiency . . . These opportunities must focus on development of understandings and on relationships among concepts and between conceptual and procedural aspects of a problem." Standards-based math programs teach students to look for patterns and generalize as opposed to expecting only computational proficiency. For example, we ask students to find a pattern that describes a relationship among a series of numbers: . . . 14, 24, 34, 44. . . . Saul (2006) suggests that teachers restate problems such as "8 + 3 = . . . " to "8 + 3 is the same as. . . . " The change in language leads children to a greater mathematical understanding: the = sign means more than just a procedure. We pose leading questions and ask students to write and draw to help organize their thinking and then we ask them to share that thinking with others. In the process, we nudge students to recognize patterns and to see relationships among concepts.

Problem Solving

According to the NCTM *Standards* (2000, p. 182), "Problem solving is the cornerstone of school mathematics. . . . " Problem solving is not a distinct topic, but a process that should permeate the study of mathematics and provide a context in which concepts and skills are learned." In the process of discovering the solution to a problem, students develop a deeper understanding of the problem and can begin to justify their work.

Pape (2004) investigated middle school students' problem-solving behaviors from a reading comprehension perspective. He suggests that students require linguistic knowledge to accurately represent the problem and mathematical knowledge to execute a successful solution.

Talking and Writing about Math Learning

Talking and writing are ways that students develop a deep and meaningful understanding of mathematical concepts. According to the NCTM *Standards* (2000, p. 194), students are expected to "communicate their mathematical thinking coherently and clearly to peers, teachers, and others." They are expected to "analyze and evaluate the mathematical thinking strategies of others," and to "use the language of mathematics to express mathematical ideas precisely. They do so with the help of language arts. As Pape (2004) explains, students must use their linguistic knowledge as well as their mathematical knowledge to be successful in math. Whitin and Whitin (2000, p. 3) describe the talk and writing of children as "highlighting one of Vygotsky's (1978) main ideas: talking does not merely reflect thought but it generates new thoughts and new ways to think."

The five process standards recorded in the NCTM *Standards* (2000) include problem solving, reasoning and proof, connections, communication, and representation. To meet these and the mathematics content standards, students must develop the ability to think mathematically. Language arts provide the tools for teachers and students to read and understand problems, to write and draw their way toward understanding, and to communicate effectively.

COMPARING LITERACY AND MATH THINKING SKILLS

In our experience, teachers begin to see the power of math–literacy integration when they see the underlying similarities between the two areas. Students need to learn and use the same set of thinking strategies in reading, writing, or math workshops and throughout the day. These strategies include making connections, predicting, asking questions, being aware of their thinking (metacognition), making inferences, visualizing, summarizing, and determining importance.

In math lessons students make connections to link new information to what they already know. Connections support students' ability to *make predictions* about patterns they notice and about data presented in a variety of formats. They predict solutions to problems and check to see if they were right in much the same way they check their predictions when reading. They need to *ask questions* that can be addressed with data, check that the problem they are working on makes sense, and that their solutions are explainable and logical. This is especially true when using calculators. We constantly ask students if their answers make sense even while they are working on computation skills. We also ask if someone knows another way to solve the same problem so students get used to sharing their thinking and recognize that there is more than one way to think about and solve problems. We ask students to be *metacognitive* in the same way we want them to be aware of their thinking while reading and writing.

Students are often expected to *make inferences* about data when presented with mathematical information. We teach students to *visualize* when grappling with concepts and problem solving as a way to make the information more concrete before using abstract mathematical symbols. They learn to *summarize* and synthesize data when working to understand tables, graphs, diagrams, and maps. They must organize and consolidate their mathematical thinking just as they must organize and consolidate their thinking when interpreting the meaning of a particular text. They need to *determine what is important* when presented with a word problem and to understand how details are used to provide additional information and to clarify meaning. This thinking is similar to what readers do to determine the important points of an informational article, or to figure out characters' motives when reading fiction. In short, we pose problems, ask questions, present mathematical models, and ask students to reflect on their mathematical learning in much the same way that we ask them to reflect on their learning in reading and writing class. Table 1.1 shows these comparisons.

Students do not recognize math and literacy similarities by themselves. Teachers must help them see that what they do to understand a story can also be used to understand a math problem. They can connect, predict (estimate), question, visualize, reread, paraphrase, summarize, and check for understanding as they work through the problem. Then, students must organize their ideas to write a coherent explanation for how they solve a math problem in similar ways to how they must organize their ideas when writing an essay. All of this suggests the power of explicitly teaching how similar thinking strategies are used in all learning.

Maintaining the Integrity of the Disciplines

While math and literacy share a set of thinking strategies, there are important differences between them that must be addressed in teaching. Mathematics includes the use of numerals, symbols, and computational procedures that are domain specific. Students must learn to read these in order to understand math and to communicate effectively. Mathematics has its own language and specialized vocabulary. Students must learn the vocabulary and terms that underlie mathematical concepts. It is important for students to develop their own algorithms to comprehend the underlying operational concepts, even as they are directly taught the most commonly used algorithms. Having an array of strategies increases their repertoire for problem solving. Mathematical thinking becomes another way to view the world and solve real-world problems.

REFINING WHAT WE MEAN BY MATH–LITERACY INTEGRATION

When we first began thinking and talking about the integration of math and literacy, we discussed the similarities between them and thought this represented integrated instruction. However, some of the literature on the integration of math and literacy caused us to rethink our position.

Mathematics teacher educators have struggled with defining "integrated mathematics" and suggest that a diversity of definitions exist. House (2003, p. 5), quoting the findings of Lott and Reeves (1991), concluded the following:

TABLE 1.1. Comparison of Math and Literacy Learning

Math	Literacy
Make connections	**Make connections**
I can make connections to this problem by thinking about others like it that I have solved before. I can make connections between this concept and what I know from reading in science or from what I have learned about solving problems in my everyday life.	I can make connections to what I am reading by thinking of other books that I have read like this one. I can make connections to what I am reading based on experiences I have had and to what I know about the world.
Make predictions	**Make predictions**
I can make predictions about patterns, data, upcoming learning, problem solving, solutions, etc. I can make estimations. I need to check to see if predictions or estimations were correct or need revision.	I can predict what the story is about by looking at chapter titles. I can predict what characters will do next, or predict motives, plot, or resolution. I can predict themes or predict topics in nonfiction, etc. I need to check to see if predictions were correct or need revision.
Ask questions	**Ask questions**
I can ask questions about data, or for clarity, or to determine what the problem is about, and to decide if the answers and solutions make sense.	I can ask questions about story elements, characters' motives, author's purpose, to clarify meaning, and to understand the text.
Self-regulate or be metacognitive	**Self-regulate or be metacognitive**
Think about the problem: Does it make sense? Do I need to reread or restate the problem? Does the solution make sense? Can I solve the problem another way? Do I understand the math terms? Can I summarize the problem and explain my answer?	Think about the reading: Do I understand what I am reading? Do I need to reread or restate the reading in my own words? Do I have questions? Do I need clarification of the way the author is using certain words? Can I summarize what I am reading? Do I agree or disagree with the author?
Infer	**Infer**
Much like predicting, I can infer what will come next using the data presented. I can make an informed guess about additional information needed. I can infer or estimate a solution.	I can draw conclusions about the characters, setting, or solution to the main character's problem. I can infer the meaning of words using context. I can infer the author's intent or biases.
Visualizing	**Visualizing**
I can make pictures in my mind or I can draw what I think the problem is about. I can represent the different parts of the problem by drawing or diagramming the problem.	I can create pictures in my mind of the setting and the characters. I can picture the problem the characters are facing and think about how I would act to solve the problem. I can imagine what the characters are feeling and how they look and act.

(continued)

TABLE 1.1. *(continued)*

Summarize	Summarize
I can summarize the problem and explain the steps to solve the problem. I can justify the solution using logic and mathematical reasoning.	I can summarize the story, state the theme or author's intent, and can justify the interpretation of the text using examples from the text.
Determine importance	**Determine importance**
When reading math problems I can separate the important information from the supporting details. I can determine which details are used to clarify and which are not important.	When reading I can separate the main ideas from the supporting details. I can reflect on new information and can decide whether this information contributes to understanding the main points of the story or article.

An integrated mathematics program is a holistic mathematics curriculum that

> ➤ consists of topics from a wide variety of mathematical fields and blends those topics to emphasize the connections and unity among those fields;
> ➤ emphasizes the relationships among topics within mathematics as well as between mathematics and other disciplines;
> ➤ is problem centered and application based;
> ➤ emphasizes problem solving and mathematical reasoning;
> ➤ provides multiple contexts for students to learn mathematics concepts;
> ➤ provides continual reinforcement of concepts through successively expanding treatment of those concepts;
> ➤ makes appropriate use of technology.

Usiskin (2003, p. 22) suggests that connections between math and science are important, but argues that connecting math with social studies and reading is also important. However, he argues against interdisciplinary integration stating, "I believe that mathematics should not be integrated with those other areas. It is too difficult to give enough attention to the different concepts in different subjects simultaneously, yet demonstrate the differences in their importance, and also link them in some coherent way." Berlin (2003, p. 55) suggests that integration across disciplines is "embedded most often in the context of real-world applications. As such, the cross-curricular connections tend to be contextual rather than conceptual." Perhaps what is most important is to make use of the contextual opportunities to point out how students use thinking strategies, talking, reading, and writing in math class to understand, express, and record their thinking and understandings.

We are very clear about the need to provide time in the schedule for specific math instruction. We are also clear about the need for students to develop computational skills. A balance between conceptual math and traditional math with an emphasis on computation skills is necessary for students to reach the high levels of math competence expected today. Most importantly, we believe that students must find value in the study of mathematics and see how it relates to solving real-world problems.

We also know that it is necessary to teach reading and language arts in a separate block to give adequate time to developing the reading and writing competencies students need to be successful in school and beyond. Students must be directly and explicitly taught skills and strategies for decoding, vocabulary development, and comprehension. "Writing to learn" is a common phrase teachers use to explain why it is important to include writing in all of the disciplines. However, students need adequate time and explicit teaching to understand the forms and conventions of writing, to understand voice and organization, and to develop the craft of writing. Thus, we are not advocating a thematic approach to linking literacy and math, but are advocating for the explicit teaching in the math block of how to read the math text and how to write math explanations and justifications of solutions to communicate effectively. We are also advocating for the inclusion of math read-alouds and trade books in the reading block as another form of informational text reading. These texts become models for reading the math textbook and allow the teacher additional opportunities to demonstrate how to use a specific strategy or set of strategies to improve comprehension of story problems or math explanations.

Metsisto (2005, p. 11) states, "If we intend for students to understand mathematical concepts rather than to produce specific performances, we must teach them to engage meaningfully with mathematics texts." She refers to the reading demands of math classes and ends the chapter with, "Mathematics teachers should recognize that part of their job in helping their students become autonomous, self-directed learners is first to help them become strategic, facile readers of mathematics text" (p. 23).

We know that math texts present unique challenges and that students often experience difficulty understanding them. In Chapters 4 and 5 we offer strategies to help students become strategic, facile readers of mathematics text. It is, as Metsisto states, our job to help them understand the text and to help them become independent users of strategies so that they have a sense of agency for reading the text. In so doing, we are also addressing some of the English Language Arts Standards that require students to read and comprehend a variety of texts for a variety of purposes, use a variety of strategies to comprehend, interpret, and evaluate texts, employ a wide variety of strategies as they write for a variety of purposes, and adjust their use of spoken, written, and visual language to communicate effectively. Appendix B lists the complete set of English Language Arts Standards.

PLANNING FOR LITERACY AND MATH INTEGRATION

THIRD GRADER, MAGGIE: Wait . . . is this reading or is it math?

TEACHER: This is Reading Workshop! But we *are* reading about math because these scientists are using math.

THIRD GRADER, CHAD: Wow! My brain feels bigger! I use bigger words every day!

All of the teachers who worked on this book agree—the last thing we want is an extra layer of planning in our already overpacked days. The surprise is that our classroom lives actually became simpler as we focused on connecting math and literacy. The days became more cohesive because our students transferred skills and thinking from one discipline to another.

As explained above, we do not advocate teaching the day's math lesson at language arts time. What we do advocate is integration that, first, explicitly teaches students how to read the math text and effectively communicate math explanations, both verbally and in writing. Second, we advocate including math concept books in the reading block as another form of informational text. This takes planning but the planning most useful to us was brief and focused. Detailed planning for one math unit helped us identify opportunities for teaching children how to use vocabulary, talking, reading, and writing in math. Such planning also helped us identify related concept books that might be used for shared or guided reading.

Planning Math Lessons with Literacy in Mind

Classroom teachers know that math lessons present literacy challenges. Students need reading and thinking skills to comprehend word problems. They need vocabulary for math terms and for the inner dialogue students have with themselves as they solve problems. A college math student we talked with said:

"When I am thinking about a math problem or learn something new, I do not just see a bunch of numbers in my head. I talk to myself in words. I need to sort things out. Having the right vocabulary helps me make connections. I think like this: 'Hey, I don't have a clue what is going on here.' Then someone says the word *matrix*. 'Oh! I know what kind of problem this is. This is like other matrix problems!' I use language in my head to create something real out of numbers, and to take something real and put it into numbers."

For planning math lessons with literacy in mind, we identified points in the lesson where students would need an inner dialogue to read and understand problems or to learn new concepts. We also identified opportunities for students to clarify thinking through writing and talking. The thinking strategies taught in reading such as making connections, predicting, questioning, self-regulating (metacognitive), inferring, visualizing, summarizing, and determining importance (see Table 1.1) are also important in math. By connecting with these strategies throughout our day, we help students transfer the same kinds of thinking to math. One teacher found an easy way to link these. The class had created a chart listing the reading and thinking strategies the children had learned. It was displayed in the reading "corner." The teacher shifted the poster to a prominent place in the center of the room. This allowed the class to refer to the strategies throughout the day and across the curriculum. While planning the math lesson, the teacher also put sticky notes in the margins of her teacher's manuals reminding her to prompt children to use the strategies—for example, "What other problem does this remind you of? Who has a connection?"

One of our goals for literacy in our math classes is to encourage the process of inquiry. We want to build an environment where inquiry is the norm and by including inquiry in the math class, we move closer to achieving our goal. We want our students to understand that they learn from each other as they talk together about what they know and figure out. As Johnston (2004, p. 52) writes, "The more we help children build a sense of themselves as inquirers and problem-solvers, and the less they see boundaries between domains of inquiry, the more they are likely to transfer their learning into the world beyond school." So we plan to build in opportunities like the Inquiry example in Chapter 3.

Adding Math Content during Literacy Lessons

We recommend adding mathematics content to what students are reading, writing, and talking about during literacy lessons. When we began to do this we were amazed! "My *math* lessons seem to unfold so easily," one teacher noted. Math lessons suddenly take a lot less time! This happens because we are building background knowledge in advance of the lesson. When teaching vocabulary from literature, science, and social studies we add words for upcoming math lessons. By preteaching some of the vocabulary we "frontload" a lot of mathematical information. We also use shared- reading texts with math content as we teach reading strategy lessons and, about once a week, we include a math writing prompt in our writing workshop. This activates and adds to knowledge children will use later in math lessons. Planning for integration is not cumbersome; it simply requires awareness of using math as a context for practicing language competencies. Math–literacy integration, however, needs to take the daily classroom schedule into account. Where does it fit?

Daily Schedules

Most school districts specify the number of minutes for instruction in the major content areas. Our district recommends 60 minutes daily for math instruction depending on the grade level. The district also requires that teachers set aside 90–120 minutes for reading instruction and 40 minutes for language arts instruction.

We also have daily time set aside for physical education and four days of the week students rotate through library, drama, art, and music. This leaves limited time for science and social studies. We currently use a science program that requires teachers to rotate through three to four units, each with lots of hands-on experiences coupled with text-based instruction. Therefore, to get enough minutes to adequately address the topics in science and social studies, we must integrate them with language arts instruction. We will use Carole Skalinder's fall schedule to illustrate how we find the time for this integration. Figure 1.1 shows Carole's daily schedule and represents her effort to create a coherent structure whereby the teacher and students can make connections across content.

Carole labels much of her day as "workshop," and students know there is a routine to how workshop time will be spent. The workshop format supports the notion of apprenticeship and provides comfort for students to predict how the day will progress. The routines of workshop typically include a whole-group mini-lesson followed by small-group instruction followed by independent practice or working with peers (Dorn & Soffos, 2001).

In Reading Workshop 1, Carole typically introduces a reading or vocabulary strategy by reading aloud or by enlarging the text or putting it on the overhead so all of the students can see the text while she models how to use the strategy. After the mini-lesson, Carole meets with students in small, guided reading groups to apply the same strategy on appropriately challenging text. However, Carole occasionally uses a math informational book or the math textbook for a whole-class strategy lesson before using the same type of text in guided reading. As another example, during the beginning of the year when scaffolding of solving word problems focuses on *reading* the problems, she might use Reading Workshop time to do a shared reading of a math word problem and then provide guided practice in small groups. During the time of the year when the *writing* part of problem solving is emphasized, she uses some of the Writers' Workshop time for shared writing lessons and guided practice of the skills and strategies needed for writing explanations and solutions to math problems.

During Math Workshop, Carole might introduce the whole-class math lesson by reading aloud a math-related book to create a context for the rest of the lesson. Depending on the lesson and concepts being taught, she may then guide students to use talk and writing as a way of further exploring the concept or strategy. This time slot is primarily devoted to explicit teaching of the math curriculum. Ideally, Carole would have one continuous Math Workshop. However, she must work around the schedule for physical education and resume the Math Workshop later. Carole's challenge was to set up the workshop so that the interruption would occur at the conclusion of the whole-group lesson and not interrupt students' work. The second portion of the Math Workshop includes independent practice of the concept presented earlier. During this time Carole also works with individuals who need further guidance in understanding and applying the concepts and strategies presented earlier. In the afternoon, Carole designates a 20-minute mini-block,

	Mon	Tue	Wed	Thu	Fri
9:00–9:15	**Homework connections**—students check in homework/revisit, review, ask questions **Daily geography/Word Study/Vocabulary/Poetry**				

9:15–10:30	**Reading Workshop 1**
	 Shared reading/mini-lesson
	 Small-group instruction:
	   guided reading
	   book discussions
	   assisted writing
	   individual or small-group
	   conferencing
	 Choice reading				

10:30–11:15	**Math Workshop** Whole-group lesson				
11:15–11:35	**Physical Education**				
11:35–12:00	**Math Workshop** Students pick up Math Homelinks Guided/independent practice				
12:00–12:40	**Recess/Lunch**				
12:40–1:10	**Reading Workshop 2** Read aloud/independent wide reading Small-group instruction Individual or small-group conferencing				

Time					
1:10–1:30	Math Workshop 2	Math Workshop 2	Math Writing	Math Workshop 2	Math Workshop 2
1:30–2:10	**Writers' Workshop** Read aloud/mini-lesson Grammar/mechanics/word study, spelling Independent writing, teacher conferencing	**Writers' Workshop** Read aloud/mini-lesson Grammar/mechanics/word study, spelling Independent writing, teacher conferencing	**Inquiry Workshop** Science/Social Studies research Independent reading, writing, teacher conferencing, guided inquiry	**Science/Social Studies** Lesson **Inquiry Workshop** Science/Social Studies research Independent reading, writing, teacher conferencing, guided inquiry	**Writers' Workshop** Read aloud/mini-lesson Grammar/mechanics/word study, spelling Independent writing, teacher conferencing
2:10–2:20					
2:20–2:30	Read Aloud	Read Aloud	Read Aloud		Read Aloud
2:30–3:10	Library	Art	Music		Library
3:10–3:20	Dismissal				

FIGURE 1.1. Mrs. Skalinder's third-grade schedule, Fall 2006.

called "Math Workshop 2," to be used four days per week for math games and problem-solving investigations. This system has allowed Carole to regularly provide time for students to work independently and in partnerships. She uses this time for math centers, which will be elaborated on later in this chapter in the section on setting up a language-rich math environment. Finally, Carole devotes the same time block one day per week for explicit and extended math talk or math writing.

Figuring out whether math literacy experiences get taught in the Math Workshop or in the Reading or Writers' Workshop requires constant monitoring and reflection about the pacing in each discipline and the current needs and readiness levels of the students. To simplify this and to help us focus on, math–literacy links, we created a Math–Literacy Planning Sheet. It was essential for us that this sheet be easy to use, flexible, and require a minimum of writing.

The Math–Literacy Planning Sheet

We start our planning for math–literacy integration by identifying the key learning standards and/or benchmarks that are part of the math lesson or unit, and then find connections with literacy standards being addressed in other parts of the day. We note the literacy demands of upcoming math lessons and enter them on the planning sheet as math–literacy objectives. A sample planning sheet for Carole's third-grade math unit on multidigit subtraction is shown in Figure 1.2. We focused on four literacy skill areas that are important to math learning: vocabulary, talking, reading, and writing. Specific activities that we have used to link math and literacy are described in Chapters 2 through 7 of this book, grouped into the four main categories on the planning sheet.

Once the math objectives are clear, we use the planning sheet to list the activities and address them in the left column. Then we list the mini-lessons and practice sessions where these activities can be integrated into daily lessons in the right column. The following list of ideas helped us as we began to organize our thinking. We wanted to incorporate a wide range of strategies and resources for differentiating instruction to address students' range of learning styles as we planned a 2- to 4-week unit.

➢ Think of ways students can actively enjoy exploring the concepts. Do we have varied learning resources and written material? Collect trade books, CD-ROMs, related fiction, and websites. Locate multiple levels of materials.

➢ Teach vocabulary: activate prior knowledge. Highlight words in the unit through stories. Have children write definitions, take notes, and make anchor charts. Add the words to the word wall and spelling list, and use them to create concept sorts.

➢ Identify reading, writing, and talk expectations. Use them as you ask students to think critically and to express themselves in written and oral form.

Unit Subtraction Grade 3	Integration
Math Vocabulary *Preteach vocabulary* Word Think Sheet	Introduce and model in word study Practice in literacy centers Reinforce in math class
Math Talk *Partner talk* Introduce "Turn-and-Talk Clock" Prompt: What would the world be like without math?" Teacher circulates, reports afterward about hearing "What do you think?" Children take turns circulating (also listen for math vocabulary)	Introduce and practice in math game mini-block
Math Reading *Visualizing: flow charts/diagrams* Visualize sequence for solving subtraction word problems Shared reading: use "water cycle" flow chart from science Children create flow charts using word problems from math lesson as texts	Introduce and model in math class Reinforce and practice in reading strategy lesson
Math Writing Writing Poetry Children write and illustrate "List Poems" (See *Teaching Children Mathematics*, Altieri, 2005, p. 21)	Reinforce and revisit in writing workshop

FIGURE 1.2. Math–literacy planning sheet—third grade.

> ➢ Use these student expressions as assessments along the way to help adjust instruction.

A Sample Math–Literacy Planning Sheet for Third-Grade Subtraction

Carole's planning sheet for a third-grade math unit on multidigit subtraction is shown in Figure 1.2. While all the boxes on this planning sheet are filled, it is not necessary to do this much planning right away! We encourage teachers to begin with just one or two entries. When we started focusing on integration in our own classrooms we selected one area at a time. For example, we might have used only the math vocabulary box for several weeks in a row, establishing a routine, and doing the same type of vocabulary activity once each week. It is fine to start by giving students (and the teacher) one or two good opportunities to experience math–literacy connections, in which case several boxes on the planning sheet would be left blank. The following sections explain Carole's planning sheet.

Math Vocabulary

Carole wanted to preteach vocabulary for the multidigit subtraction unit and so she planned and started this activity about five weeks prior to the teaching of the unit. She made a list of vocabulary words for the unit and decided to put six words each week into the class spelling (word study) lists during the time leading up to the unit. She planned to build background knowledge by using a "Word Think Sheet." This form asks students to think about a specific vocabulary word by drawing a picture, thinking of related words, using the target word in a sentence, and finally, expressing the word's meaning. The sheet is the basis for an exercise in shared thinking and for writing lessons during vocabulary instruction time. Once Carole's students were familiar with the Word Think Sheet, they could complete several more of them independently at centers during their literacy block. We will describe the Word Think Sheet's use in detail in Chapter 6.

Math Talk

To help the class strengthen their productive math talk with partners, Carole introduced the "Turn-and-Talk Clock." This activity is a scaffolding tool for student conversations. A question is asked and the children are given a short time to talk about it with a partner. (See Chapter 2 for a fuller description.) Carole decided to introduce the activity in the math game mini-block (Math Workshop 2 on Carole's schedule), using a general prompt: "What would the world be like without math?" She specifically wanted to teach partners to ask each other, "What do you think?" After introducing the Turn-and-Talk Clock, Carole would circulate and listen briefly to conversations, then let students know what she heard. She could point out examples where she had heard partners asking each other, "What do you think?" After a little practice during explicit teaching in Math Workshop 2 (see Figure 1.1), the class could use this strategy during the math lesson. Carole knew she could identify places in any lesson where children would benefit from turning and talking briefly about a concept, word, or problem. On the Math–Literacy Planning Sheet she also noted that students might take turns circulating and listening to conversations, using the teacher's behavior as a model. They could then report to the whole group about what they heard. Carole planned one more idea to keep in the back of her mind and use if the class were ready to do a little more: She could prompt students to notice anyone using good math vocabulary.

Reading

Third-grade students often need support for reading and comprehending word problems about subtraction situations. "Tom had $24.00. He spent $13.00 on gold-fish supplies. How much does he have now?" For a problem like this, it helps students to draw a picture such as a flow chart, showing what the situation was at first, what happened, and what the outcome was. Carole planned to use a few minutes of math time to introduce this visualizing strategy as they read and solved problems. Knowing they would need to learn about flow charts and diagrams for reading nonfiction in general, she planned a shared reading lesson to focus on visualizing. They could examine and discuss flow diagrams from science- and social studies-related texts in the reading series. Children could then practice drawing their own flow charts and diagrams using math word problems.

Writing

At Carole's school there was a year-long focus on writing poetry, so the class returned to it frequently in Writers' Workshop. Carole planned to use a suggestion for "List Poetry" from *Teaching Children Mathematics* (Altieri, 2005). Children would choose a favorite number and then write about various ways the number is used, creating a poem in the form of a list. While planning, Carole recognized that this idea could be introduced quickly to third graders as part of a writing mini-lesson. She could read them several examples and then let them write and illustrate their own poems. She wrote "Writers' Workshop" on the planning sheet, knowing it could be either a single assignment for the whole class or one of several topics the children would choose from for that week. While not included on the Math–Literacy Planning Sheet, Carole and the rest of the authors plan for independent practice of the math concepts taught during workshop by using math centers. They are included here because they relate to schedules and require planning in order to occur regularly and to be beneficial to students.

Math Centers

We all agree that it is important for students to have time to explore mathematics in a less structured environment than during the formal math lesson. We all use math centers but each of us uses them differently.

Patti Satz includes math as one of the centers available to her second-grade students during center time. She initially experimented with having math center as part of the math lesson but she found that only the students who finished the practice portion of the lesson regularly got to the math center. Therefore, she changed to her current structure so that all students would have the opportunity to participate in the math center activities. The math activities in the center are usually related to the season of the year and may also be related to other areas being studied. For example, each student made a place value building that went on "Place Value Lane" in November. When they study fractions, each student makes a sundae with each scoop of ice cream identified as a fraction. Patti has a variety of other centers going at the same time: listening center, writing center, reading center, and a word work center. Students choose a center and mark a ticket to remember what centers they worked at. While at the center, they record their work in their log.

Carole has experimented with a variety of schedules and groupings to include centers and independent time for math investigations. She currently organizes her third-grade students into five heterogeneous groups that stay the same for a couple of months. The student groups are assigned to a particular area of the room for center time. The groups have labeled tubs on a shelf that they pick up and take to their assigned work space. This works well because the students often leave their work in the tubs until they are finished. This system allows Carole to check on each student's work and the progress toward completion without having to search through other student work. Carole rotates the activities that are in the tubs. Each tub has Velcro-attached labels so she can easily change the activities in the tubs by simply changing the labels. During the time the students are working, Carole works with individuals or groups, or pulls out particular students to work on something else.

Summary and Implications

Teachers have the awesome responsibility of providing a challenging curriculum and powerful instruction that engages students and enables them to be successful in school and in life. In *Reading to Learn* (2002, p. 172), Allington and Johnston describe lessons from exemplary fourth-grade classrooms. The teachers they studied all integrated their instruction. Reading and writing were most often "emphasized as a tool in the study of other subjects." However, math was the least commonly integrated subject. We hope this book will help change that.

We are not only using language arts as tools in the study of mathematics, but are also helping students to meet standards in both disciplines. We believe that the ideas and strategies presented in this book can help students achieve more and become successful in middle school and beyond. In the chapters that follow, we offer practical strategies for integrating mathematics and literacy learning. In Chapters 2 and 3, we offer strategies and ideas for encouraging children to talk about math and learn math through talking. Getting children talking about math is a foundation for many of the other teaching activities that follow. In Chapters 4 and 5 we discuss the reading challenges presented by many math texts and how to address them successfully. This includes using literature with math content to prepare students and explicitly teaching them how to read and understand math problems. Chapter 6 offers a range of strategies for teaching math terms and concepts. As you will see, a great deal of writing is embedded in the various activities in all of the chapters, but writing is highlighted in Chapter 7. We end with a discussion of assessment. In the balance of this chapter, we offer suggestions for setting up a language-rich math classroom.

SETTING UP A LANGUAGE-RICH MATH CLASSROOM

The following are ideas on how to set up a language-rich math classroom. These suggestions are aimed at creating a culture that allows students to be active learners and show respect for ideas and for each other. In this kind of atmosphere, mistakes are considered opportunities to learn, risk taking is celebrated, and mathematics is presented as a way of thinking and exploring, and as a way to solve problems encountered in our daily lives.

Word Walls

We immerse students in the vocabulary of mathematics by using the walls and classroom space as reminders of the words under study or learned in previous units. Blachowicz, Fisher, Ogle, and Watts-Taffe (2006, p. 528) validate this practice. "Research studies in diverse contexts and with learners of varying ages all confirm that environments where language and word use are celebrated and noted encourage the development of word consciousness and attendant vocabulary learning." Math is a technical language that is not always integrated into a student's vocabulary and it must be if they are to communicate orally and in writing about their thinking and problem solving. Thus, the words are posted on the wall to remind students of the terms and to provide easy access for use in talk and writing. Math words are often kept on a separate chart with the unit of study at the top to help students categorize them by topic. In her fifth-grade classroom, Sandy Vitantonio includes a description and picture along with the word itself to help math language become a permanent part of her students' vocabulary. In her third-grade classroom, Carole keeps math words currently under study on a separate "mini-word wall" and then moves the words to the main word wall when the unit is over. A part of Carole's word wall is shown in Figure 1.3. She also includes some of the math words on the main word wall if they demonstrate the spelling patterns under study.

Number Lines

Number lines are placed on the wall in continuous order. Even if the number line is broken up by a doorway, it continues around the upper perimeter of the room.

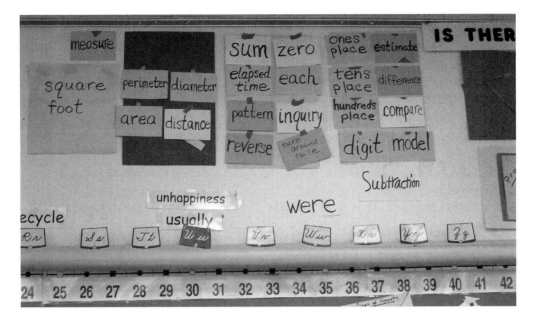

FIGURE 1.3. Word wall and number line.

The number line, like the word wall, is continually used by teachers as they demonstrate how to solve problems and to understand the order of numbers. When teachers notice that a student has used one of these resources, they will ask the student to tell the class how he or she figured out a solution. By helping students make public their use of these resources, we remind other students of their value.

Anchor Charts

Anchor charts such as the one shown in Figure 1.4 summarize a process or procedure for approaching a task, for solving particular kinds of problems, or for working through the text. They are co-constructed with students and serve as reminders of how to proceed or what to do when presented with a particular kind of text. For example, we create anchor

FIGURE 1.4. The children and teacher made an anchor chart about what to do when they are confused.

charts for how to choose a "just right" book, for how to solve problems, and to recount steps in a process for writing math explanations, among other uses. We say more about anchor charts in Chapter 2.

Math Words in the Real World

Along with math vocabulary and anchor charts, there should be visible connections of math to the real world. For her second-grade class, Patti set up a bulletin board with the question: "Where's the Math?" posted over pictures that changed weekly. Figure 1.5 shows what the board looks like. Soon, students began bringing in their own pictures to show how math is connected to many aspects of their lives.

Many teachers have number words spelled out and on display in the classroom: under number lines, on place-value charts, on calendars, and placed next to routines for the day. This provides students with sight word recognition of important math terms that are not always easy to spell or sound out (e.g., *one*," "*two*," "*four*," "*eight*," "*eleven*," "*twelve*," "*thirteen*," "*fifteen*," "*twenty*," "*thirty*," "*forty*," and "*fifty*"). Lisa uses library pockets adhered to poster board in her third-grade class-

FIGURE 1.5. This interactive bulletin board gets second graders thinking about math in the real world.

room to keep track of borrowed books from the classroom library. Each pocket is labeled with a spelled-out number: "seven," "eight," "nine," and so on.

Labeling Classroom Objects with Math Terms

Lisa also suggests that students describe and/or label items in the classroom using their mathematical vocabulary: a tabletop can be identified as a square, circle, or rectangle, a can might be labeled as a cylinder, and the globe can be labeled as a sphere. This practice is especially helpful for English language learners (ELLs). Student-created displays help students take ownership of the terms connected with the unit of study. Lisa asks students to find pictures or objects to display on a poster or bulletin board that represent the math concept under study. Students label the picture or object using the appropriate math terms to reinforce their use and to provide another opportunity to write the words. Figure 1.6 shows a student-made poster for the term *symmetry*. Since the students create the display, they are likely to notice and use the words in their talk and writing.

Hands-On Materials

The NCTM *Principles and Standards* (2000) state that teaching practices need to increase the use of manipulatives. Manipulatives can be any material—from pieces of paper to base-10 blocks to dice—that can be manipulated or rearranged by students to represent a problem or understand a concept. They serve as concrete objects for students to use as they solve problems and conceptualize abstract ideas. Manipulatives allow students to visualize concepts and to make concrete connections to problems: they "see" problem solving. Most published mathematics programs come with a supply list. Often, manipulatives are purchased by school districts when a program is adopted for classroom use. However, if this is not the case, Figure 1.7 provides a list of items that are needed in most elementary math programs.

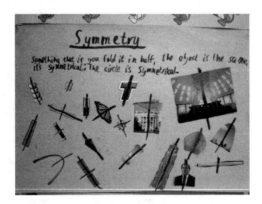

FIGURE 1.6. Students' illustrated examples of *symmetry*.

Calculators (age appropriate)	Yardsticks and metric sticks
Base-10 blocks	Tape measures
Geometric pattern blocks	Trundle wheel
Clocks	Scales and balances
100 chart	Measurement containers (e.g., cups, pints, quarts, gallons)
Number lines	
Calendars	Geoboards
Playing cards	Rubberbands
Dice (numbered, blank, 6-sided, 12-sided, 20-sided)	Coin stamps
	Play money
Spinners	Fraction sticks
Probability meter	Geometric solids
Percentage circles	Graph paper
Compasses	Writing journals
Protractors	
Rulers	

FIGURE 1.7. Manipulatives and supplies needed in most elementary math programs. Many of the manipulatives come as an overhead for instruction (e.g., geoboards, pattern blocks, coins).

As you will see from the activities in this book, writing has a significant role in a language-based math program. Thus, we include writing journals on the list of materials. The journals can be put on student supply lists or included in the school budget. Many of our teachers use theme books and train students not to remove pages so that the journal serves as a portfolio of students' yearly writing and problem-solving progress in math. We keep a section of the journal for students to record new math vocabulary and definitions. Some teachers use three-ring binders to serve the same purpose and to store student work. The teacher must decide if the journals are to be stored in the students' desks or on shelves.

Since manipulatives are central to mathematics study in the elementary grades, they must be placed so that they are accessible to students and packaged in such a way that they can be easily replaced to be used again. We have clearly labeled bins and plastic zip bags for storing manipulatives. Keeping the math tools and materials organized and returned to their proper place can become one of the "jobs" assigned to students. To emphasize the importance of this job, we designate a title such as "Mathematics Monitor" or "Tools Technician" and add the title to the classroom job chart. The formal job title also reminds students that the manipulatives are to be used as tools and not as toys.

Some math tools are shared and kept in a common storage area and others are personal and need to be kept in desks or in student storage containers. We suggest using plastic zip bags for personal student tools and manipulatives. We assign each student a number at the beginning of the year. The math tools and manipulatives that are for individual use are also marked with the student's number. Numbers can be designated by alphabetical order of the students' last names. This system makes it easy to return a stray straightedge or an eraser to the rightful owner because the objects have numbers on them. Students can also be asked to place the same number on the top of their work along with their names. Students love putting papers in numerical order and this makes it easy for the teacher to see who is missing an assignment.

Decks of cards can become a challenge if there is a lone card left on the floor and no one remembers which deck it fell out of. We suggest using colors and symbols to keep track of decks of cards. For example, one deck might have a small red circle on the top of every card. Another deck might have a small green triangle on the top. Although it takes time to mark each card in each deck, doing so will help these tools last from year to year.

When a classroom is physically set up to be rich in math language, the next step is getting the children to start talking math. Chapter 2 offers guidelines for how to do that.

GETTING CHILDREN STARTED ON MATH TALK

The *Principles and Standards for School Mathematics* (NCTM, 2000, p. 52) tells us that problem solving should be integrated with all mathematics learning. Further, students need to evaluate, analyze, and communicate their thinking clearly and precisely "to peers, teachers, and others" (2000, p. 60). Because of these standards and others, we are freed from old myths:

➤ Myth: Only right answers count.

➤ Myth: Only teachers know.

➤ Myth: It is important for students to do their own work—never share.

Liberated from the old assumptions, how do we help ourselves and our students use dialogue more effectively? This chapter and the next examine math talk in two phases: "Getting Started" and "Getting Better." We present examples of how classes at different grade levels start with simple talking activities and move to quite sophisticated discourse.

WHAT DOES PRODUCTIVE MATH TALK LOOK LIKE?

While all school cultures promote productive learning environments, some have expectations for prevailing silence and others acknowledge the value of interaction and motion around the classroom. When students' talking is expected, how is ordinary classroom hubbub transformed into productive discourse? What do we mean by *productive discourse*?

Here is what children do in a mathematics-talking classroom:

➢ Become excited
➢ Listen to each other, ask questions, and respond to each other's ideas
➢ Support peers' thinking and understandings
➢ Work together to solve problems
➢ Expect math to make sense and try to explain the unexpected
➢ Show confidence as they take risks
➢ Adapt and invent
➢ Value and use errors
➢ Know that exchanging ideas with others is a learning strategy

Here is what successful teachers do in a mathematics-talking classroom:

➢ Maintain and convey a vision of the classroom as a community of discourse
➢ Provide mathematical explanations and guidance
➢ Provide supported opportunities for math talk
➢ Observe, listen, and question
➢ Assess discourse, provide "just right" challenges, and give students increasing responsibility
➢ Provide multiple layers of support for children who come from classrooms where talking is not expected
➢ Connect talking competencies in other curriculum areas to math discourse
➢ Show the value of students' ideas and guide lessons that are framed by them
➢ Make children's thinking visible and public (writing/talking)

Like any other aspect of the curriculum, productive conversation does not happen automatically or immediately. The above lists provide the criteria we use as we design lessons. We teach math talk beginning with explicit instruction about how to talk and listen productively. We discuss reasons why math talk is important.

➢ Math talk helps *you* understand math.
➢ Math talk helps *listeners* understand.
➢ Math talk helps *everyone* understand better.

We model these principles by taking a sample problem and by using a "fishbowl" technique. In the fishbowl, the teacher and a group of students first demonstrate the activity for the rest of the class. A small group of students sit with the teacher and talk about the problem while the rest of the class listens. Next we provide guided practice. The teacher divides the class into small groups and assigns one student from the teacher-led group to each small group. This provides support in each group as one member has already participated in the activity. A new problem is given to each group to discuss and the teacher observes the talk that follows. Initially, only a few minutes are allowed for the talk. The teacher then brings the whole class together to reflect on the activity and the talk productivity. Creating an anchor chart of what went well and what needs work provides additional support to remind students of how to talk and listen when working on problems in groups. We highlight bits of conversations that went well and remind students that we expect the talk about math to make sense. We gradually increase the amount of time for group talk as students become better at building on each other's ideas, asking questions, and sharing alternative models for problem solving.

Each new class presents a different learning community, and although it typically seems that *this* is the year the talking is *not* going to work, we persist, and it *always* develops. It is extremely important for the teacher to believe that the effort to develop productive talk will be worthwhile—and then it will be!

In the beginning we expect some difficulties. Our plan is to use children's classroom talk to teach them how to get better at purposeful conversation. Disagreements can become settings for modeling problem solving. Confusion can signal the need for everyone to understand the problem or task before starting. Vague, unfocused speech becomes the motivation to clarify thinking. All of these difficulties can arise when children are given opportunities for independent discourse, no matter how skillfully the teacher has prepared her- or himself, the students, and the setting. We go back to the fishbowl technique often to model and we provide many opportunities for guided practice after each fishbowl activity. That way we continually support students' progress.

As math talk develops the teacher will give up some control. The classroom will be louder, but if the conversation is about math and making connections, what could be better? After many experiences with math conversation, students begin to realize that mathematics is not just about arriving at the right answer. The process of *how* they get there is equally important. Instead of saying "I just know," they begin to describe their thinking.

Math talk may be planned for any part of the lesson, and should become a daily endeavor. It can be used to introduce a math concept but can also be used in other ways. Many times math talk occurs during a problem-solving exercise or when students are explaining their strategies after a math investigation. Often it is appropriate to provide guided practice by having students turn to each other and discuss an idea or a question for a few minutes. Then they refocus as a whole class to share those ideas or continue the lesson. Many times the opportunity to talk to a partner not only encourages thinking and reflection but releases energy so students can remain engaged in math talk for a longer period of time.

Discussions may include the whole class, a small group, or pairs of students sharing ideas. As the teacher plans a unit, thought should be given to placing students in groups of three or four. When interesting topics emerge, students will be ready to talk in small groups. This is an opportunity for the teacher to circulate, provide guidance, and assess students' understanding of the lesson content. The teacher may wish to have one student report each group's discussion, so that the whole class can summarize the main ideas. Keeping a brisk pace during the sharing is necessary to ensure that all groups have a chance to share.

In examining how each new class begins to develop math discourse, we identify three areas that need to be supported. They are (1) listening and speaking; (2) making sense, or clarifying thinking; and (3) risk taking for problem solving. Following are activities we have used in each of these areas.

TEACHING LISTENING AND SPEAKING

In *Shaping Literate Minds*, Dorn and Soffos (2001, pp. 7–8) define *scaffold* as "a temporary support that teachers create to help children extend current skills and knowledge to a higher level of competence." This concept guides us as we help children practice the skills of academic talking and listening. We continuously monitor class progress and provide a variety of activities as scaffolds to support growth in listening and talking.

Explicitly Teaching the Reasons for Talking

When we first introduce talking activities, we take a few minutes to tell children explicitly why we expect them to become competent math talkers.

➢ The worlds of work and of higher education emphasize team problem solving.

➢ We know that students learn more when they talk about what they are learning and thinking.

➢ Some people believe that we learn a little bit when we read, more when we listen, and even more when we discuss; but we learn the most when we teach something to someone else. Try this out. What do you think?

It is helpful for the teacher to let children know specifically which talking/listening skill will be the focus for that lesson.

"Today I will observe your groups and take notes every time I notice someone [for example]:
➢ listening to someone else."
➢ saying, 'What do you think?' "

➢ making eye contact."

➢ paraphrasing their partner's idea."

Math Circles: Building Confidence for Offering Contributions (K–Sixth Grade)

The first day of school is not a moment too soon to begin math talk! To encourage an atmosphere for meaningful math talk in her second grade, Patti uses an activity she calls "Math Circles." It teaches children to listen to others and reinforces the expectation that everyone's thoughts are needed. This powerful activity takes 2 to 3 minutes, and Patti begins immediately at the start of school.

Students sit in a circle and the teacher provides the starting point for the activity by suggesting something like, "If I were a number, I would be _____." As each student reacts with the first thing that comes to mind, everyone practices using good listening skills. The teacher reminds them to listen carefully. If a student cannot think of a response, the teacher tells him or her to take another minute to think, but remembers to return to that student at the end of the round for a response. Depending on the grade level and the confidence of the children, the teacher might accept all answers, or might require that each response be different from the others. The entire activity takes only a short time, but it promotes a sense of community and a positive feeling for children that their comments are important.

It sometimes surprises students to find that they are expected to have a voice in math class. Later on, this activity provides a flexible tool for differentiating, because each student responds at his or her level. For example, the teacher says, "Tell me another name for eight." One student said, "4 + 4." Others responded by saying, "20 – 12," and "2 + 2 + 2 + 2." Less confident students benefit from hearing ideas and vocabulary modeled by others; stronger ones get a chance to try out their extended thinking. Every student is able to contribute at his or her level of understanding and should be congratulated for responding.

Talking-and-Listening Sticks: Listening to Prepare for Extending the Talk (K–Sixth Grade)

This is a great partner activity and is very helpful for developing effective math talk skills. At the beginning of the year, Patti assigns her second graders to work in pairs. But later on, as the students get to know each other, she lets them select partners themselves.

The teacher presents a topic for students to talk about. For example, "How do you use math at holidays?" While one student talks, the other holds three popsicle sticks and listens. After 1 to 2 minutes (a 2-minute timer may be used) the talker stops. The listener then tells one idea he or she heard and places one stick on the table. When the listener has told three ideas heard from the other student's talk and laid down all three sticks, the positions are reversed. The simple device of the stick is a reminder to listen carefully and helps children recall each other's ideas.

Guided Practice: Building on Everyday Classroom Talk (K–Sixth Grade)

Many children do not expect anyone except the teacher to hear what they say, so we frequently ask our students to restate what others have just said in ordinary classroom talk. "What did Henry just say?" "Who can repeat Henry's statement in your own words?" Then, as children become accustomed to listening carefully and gain confidence in sharing their ideas, they find themselves responding to what others have said and the talk grows. At this point, the teacher can ask questions like: "Who agrees?" "Does anyone have a question about what Beth just said?" "Does anyone disagree?"

Turn-and-Talk Clock: Developing Thoughtful Conversations about Specific Topics (K–Fourth Grade)

Carole establishes talking partnerships between children who are seated next to one another and changes the partnerships monthly by rearranging the desks in her third-grade classroom. At frequent intervals during a lesson she asks students to "turn and talk" to their partners. Because one class had a lot of difficulty with this, Carole created the "Turn-and-Talk Clock" (see Figure 2.1). The "clock" is simply a circle divided into two sections. One is labeled "Listen, Think" and the other is labeled "Talk." An arrow attached in the center can be moved to point to either side.

Carole introduced the clock with the arrow pointing to "Listen, Think."

"Are you ready? Get ready . . . here comes an important question. I'm going to check on how well you talk about it with your partner. . . . Don't start yet. . . . Listen . . . Ready? When I change the pointer to 'Talk,' here's what you will talk about: How can you tell which side of the ruler is inches and which side is centimeters? . . . OK, take a minute to think about it. . . . Don't talk yet. . . . Think . . . Ready? OK . . . Now . . . Talk about that with your partner."

She then changed the arrow to point to "Talk."

The clock was well loved by the class that prompted its invention. They reminded her to use it if she forgot. The clock helped them to focus on listening carefully to what they were supposed to talk about, and then to structure their conversations accordingly. Carole has continued to use it with subsequent classes.

As partners talk, the teacher circulates around the room to listen. At first she or he

FIGURE 2.1. The "Turn-and-Talk Clock" helps children to have focused conversation during a lesson.

allows only a very short time for the conversations. As children get better at talking, the time is extended. The teacher rings a bell to call them back and briefly reports what she or he heard.

> "I heard Chad say, 'I look at the numbers and then see how big the spaces are.' I heard Troy say, 'That's a good idea.' "

The teacher compliments the partnerships where both children used the opportunity to speak *and* listen.

Over time, children move more easily and frequently in and out of partner talking as part of the flow of whole-group lessons and they sustain conversations for longer periods. Eventually they no longer need the clock in order to turn and talk.

Math Partners: Using Partnerships to Understand Another's Perspective (K–Sixth Grade)

Hufferd-Ackles, Fuson, and Sherin (2004) studied the development of the math-talk learning community, referring to it as "a classroom in which the teacher and students use discourse to support the mathematical learning of all participants" (p. 82). Data from their study led them to point out that, in order to help each other, children needed "an awareness of their own understanding and they needed to understand one another's perspectives" (p. 110).

Children need continued guidance about how to help each other in math class. Helping does not mean one student doing the work for another. Instead, it is a reciprocal effort that benefits both partners. We let children know from the very beginning of the year that they will learn how to help one another. A good way to start is to teach them that the helper should listen to and retell the other's explanations in his or her own words. The Talking-and-Listening-Sticks activity described previously can help prepare students to form effective working partnerships where both students are challenged to clarify and understand each other. The helper can then begin with what the other knows and thinks and make appropriate suggestions. In the following excerpt, we see how a helper and partner solved a problem together in a first-grade classroom.

The directions are to show different ways of making "23."

STUDENT 1: So . . . you're saying that 10 plus 10 plus 3 is 23?

STUDENT 2: Yes.

STUDENT 1: Good! Umm . . . What is another way? . . . How about combining this 10 plus 10? If we combine 10 plus 10, what would that be?

STUDENT 2: Ten plus 10 is 20.

STUDENT 1: Yes . . . um, so 20 plus what? Why don't you write it? 20 +.

STUDENT 2: (*Writes.*) 20 +.

STUDENT 1: Plus what? Twenty plus what equals 23?

STUDENT 2: (*Writes.*) 20 + 3.

STUDENT 1: Great! You got it. We did it!

The helper needs to stick with the partner until the task is completed. We suggest modeling and practicing this behavior in whole-group settings and then applying it in partnerships.

Vocabulary Eavesdropper: Supporting the Use of Accurate Vocabulary to Improve Communication (Third–Sixth Grade)

Shared vocabulary is essential for conversation. The first few times you hear students using new mathematics vocabulary naturally in conversation you will know they have truly internalized the meaning of the words.

In the Vocabulary Eavesdropper activity, the class first makes a quick list of three or four vocabulary words that pertain to the topic. The teacher records these same words on a transparency and displays them on the overhead. He or she then gives the class a prompt for discussion. One student is assigned to circulate with paper and a clipboard, "eavesdropping" on conversations.. When the "eavesdropper" hears one of the words, he or she makes a note of it, along with the context in which the word was used. Alternatively, the eavesdropper can stay seated while listening and take notes during a whole-class discussion. As part of a brief sharing time at the end of the activity, the eavesdropper reports about what words were used, and if possible, their context. The class learns to celebrate these successes!

Partner Reading: Questioning and Discussing while Reading (Late First–Sixth Grade)

In this activity, partners read the same math concept book, sharing a book if necessary. After reading a page silently each partner writes a question. Then they ask each other their questions and briefly discuss them. Carole first modeled the process for her third graders, then prepared an anchor chart based on one developed by Ogle and the Office of Public School Literacy, Chicago Board of Education (2006). This Anchor Chart for Partner Reading is shown in Figure 2.2. Carole found that her third graders could successfully do this activity together even early in the year because the task is specific and the procedure is clearly outlined.

Partner reading allows the teacher to create a center using math concept trade books that have a variety of text structures and features. Students choose a center with the concept book title that sounds most interesting. A. Rodgers and E. Rodgers (2004) describe more fully the benefits of partner reading and provide additional procedures and possible anchor charts for what the reader and listener both do during partner reading.

- Sit next to your partner.
- Read one page silently.
- Write a question.
- Read the page aloud together. Ask each other the questions.
- Talk about your answers.
- Go to the next page.

FIGURE 2.2. Anchor chart for partner reading (third grade).

Student conversations consisted of questions posed in their journals and brief, focused answers. In the following example, the children were reading *Big Bend Adventure* (Pollard, 2004), which compares the climates of deserts and mountains.

STUDENT 1: (*Reading the question from her journal*) Do you think this book makes sense?

STUDENT 2: Some of it makes sense.

STUDENT 1: (*Reading the question from her journal*) Which do you like, deserts or mountains?

STUDENT 2: I like the desert.

STUDENT 1: (*Reading a question directly from the text*) Which has more rain, the desert, or the mountains?

STUDENT 2: (*Looking at bar graph*) The mountains have more rain.

The simple structure of this exercise allowed the students to take responsibility for their reading and talking partnerships. We will talk more about partner and shared reading in Chapter 5.

Mathematics Games: A Context for Math Talk (First–Sixth Grade)

Games are a popular component of math class and also provide a structure for engaging math talk. Some math programs provide lots of games for children to practice skills and to explore concepts. In some schools teachers supplement with their own games. In either case, playing games for just 15 minutes a day provides children with an authentic context for math talk that is naturally adjusted to their own levels. Teachers who think that games should be used only as an extra activity to be done if there is time should reconsider. Likewise, teachers who use game-playing time to prepare for the next activity are missing out on a wonderful opportunity. We suggest walking around the classroom with a clipboard to take notes during a game session or joining in a game with a group of students. This helps the children stay focused. Many teachers are amazed at the amount of information they collect about math thinking and group dynamics.

When Patti introduces math games to second graders in the beginning of the year she selects partners to play the games. As the play begins she circulates to monitor how the games are being played. Are the students getting along? How are they handling disagreements? Are students clear when they are talking about their decisions or complaints? On relatively rare occasions, if students are playing the game incorrectly, the teacher needs to address the misinformation.

In third grade, Carole's game groups are composed of four or five children who stay together for a month or two. She uses different criteria in assigning groups, including considering the social and academic needs of the students at that point in time. Usually, teachers find that student groups of varying mathematics levels are the easiest to manage.

When math games are played on a regular basis as a classroom routine, the practical issues of management provide opportunities for ongoing instruction about talking and listening. It becomes obvious to the class that they need to learn how to manage their groups independently, because the teacher cannot be with each group to solve problems. Brainstorming together, doing shared writing to record ideas, and having children write in their journals are all ways to approach independent learning. One of Carole's recent third-grade classes talked and wrote for several days about game management.

A problem like, "What to do when people argue?" can produce a wealth of problem-solving ideas. Carole's third graders agreed on a system: If arguing blocks the progress of the game, everyone in the group has to stop playing and write about the problem. The teacher looks at the papers after class and the class discusses the group's problem the next day before beginning the games. Most children found they had clarified their thinking through the writing. They could also listen to one another calmly the next day, and the argument disappeared. After some time, children were heard to resolve disputes simply by saying, "Let's just not argue, because we'll only have to write about it and then start all over."

Arguments can be useful when children begin to see that the arguments are often triggered by a lack of agreement on the rules or set up of the game. When they realize this, they become motivated to clarify rules and procedures before starting. In fact, children become good at teaching games to each other. Some teachers take advantage of this as an opportunity for math talk. They introduce a new game to a few students before the lesson and then these students teach it to the other groups during the games. This serves also to help the teacher manage the setting.

One third-grade group had an argument about sharing certain equipment. With the teacher's help, the class decided where they needed to keep that equipment so each game group would have it handy. As a result, everyone knew for the rest of the year where the equipment was kept and the importance of putting it back. The class became extremely responsible about putting away materials.

Group discussions such as these about managing independently, stopping arguments, sharing equipment, and understanding instructions may arise from game playing at any grade level. They then become models for shared decision making and problem solving through talking and listening. Games or other structured small-group activities can provide the setting for diagnosing how a class functions as a group and how well they work together. These discussions and games can also be used to gradually increase the responsibility taken by students and help get them ready for the challenges of solving more abstract math problems together.

TEACHING THAT MATH MAKES SENSE

In order for productive classroom discourse to occur children need a solid awareness that math is supposed to make sense to them. Odd as it may seem to us, many children need to be taught this, and we talk about it explicitly on the first day of school. Math *is* supposed to make sense.

A class's math sense can be displayed in the response to this simplest of word problems:

Stephen got $34.00 for his birthday. He spent $12.00 on a water polo cap. How much does he have left?

The teacher asks, "What are we trying to find out?"

In an amazing number of cases, children respond, "We are trying to find out the answer." Some years, no amount of hinting or prompting can elicit a response that makes sense in the context of the problem. The class, as a group, needs experiences that help them get to the essence of a problem and learn how to act on the information provided.

Pencil Store: Providing Practice and a Real-World Context for Mathematical Interactions (Second–Third Grade)

The more children encounter authentic real-life situations that use mathematics, the more aware they are that math makes sense. Many opportunities tend to be provided in primary grades, but in later years the teacher may need to create them.

Carole's third-grade class has a store where children can purchase pencils for themselves or for the classroom. The store provides a place for clarifying math thinking and practicing dialogue in a formalized routine. Carole chooses two children at a time to be storekeepers. At first these are the students who most need practice with counting money and making change. Later she allows everyone a turn to be the storekeeper. A parent comes once a week during game time to supervise, help keep track of inventory, and keep the bag of money. In a plastic container the class houses a toy cash register, some "receipts," a few pencils, and a sign: "Fancy Pencils, $0.23." The store is open for 15 minutes during math game time. The storekeepers have a class list and quietly call "customers" one at a time. If the customers do not have money that day to purchase a pencil for themselves, the teacher gives them some money from a class fund, and they purchase a pencil or two for the classroom. The children love the store. Not only do the storekeepers have to give change, but they have to write a receipt. On the receipt they write how many pencils were purchased, the total price, and a number sentence to explain how much change was given. The students get practice giving change and they explain how they figured out the change. For something so easy to manage, the store delivers a large return as a concrete context for math and literacy!

Writing and Drawing a Model to Clarify Thinking (K–Sixth Grade)

In September, Tom, a capable third-grade math student, wrote the following problem: "Farmer Brown had 23 pigs and 17 cows. 12 horses ran away. How many did he have left?" It was hard for Tom to talk about how he solved his problem, because it did not quite make sense. The first picture he drew to go with the problem was a general illustration of a farmer with lots of pigs, cows, and horses. Tom was confused when the teacher asked, "Which ones are the horses that ran away?" When the teacher then coached him to draw a picture that represented the specific numbers of pigs and cows in the problem, he could see that there were no horses to "run away." Tom finally changed his problem to "Farmer Brown had 23 pigs and 14 cows. 8 cows ran away. How many animals did he have left?" Then he was able to explain how he solved the problem.

The example above may seem surprising, but it shows us that children need many experiences with drawing and writing in order to make sense of numbers. As our college student friend told us in Chapter 1, math is not just a bunch of numbers in our heads. It is connected to real things. This understanding is absolutely critical to students' ability to express their thinking. Writing and drawing are essential for children to link numbers to the real world. We employ both regularly to help students clarify the ideas they will use in discussions. We move back and forth between using writing to clarify thinking for talking, and using talking as a rehearsal for writing.

ENCOURAGING RISK-TAKING TALK FOR PROBLEM SOLVING

In order to have good discussions, students need interesting, nonroutine problems to talk about. To approach unfamiliar problems, they need confidence for risk taking in their mathematical thinking. The first two strategies below provide ways to assess a class's risk-taking capacity at the start of the school year. The strategies that then follow are ways to encourage children to begin to take risks in speaking up to problem solve.

"Another Way": Assessing Risk-Taking Capacity (First–Sixth Grade)

One easy way to diagnose the class's capacity for risk taking in the beginning of the year is in the context of computation. When Carole reviews subtraction at the start of the year, she presents a two- or three-digit problem such as $132 - 129 =$ ____. Usually a student volunteers to demonstrate the "regrouping" method for solving the problem. In the beginning, when the class has not yet begun to function as a group, there is not much discussion.

The children who know the procedure typically do not have much to say about it except to show that they can apply it over and over. The children who are not secure with the process hesitate to admit that they are unsure of how to do it. While reviewing subtraction, Carole asks, "Does anyone have another way of doing it?" This is a very important question for diagnosing the class as well as for eliciting discussion. We ask it many times over the course of the year. The responses become strong evidence for evaluating the class's progress as problem solvers.

When Carole asks, "Does anyone have another way to compute $132 - 129 =$ ____?" she says, "The children look at me in a most uncomfortable silence, as if I have just landed from some very strange and far away planet." But she notes what happens in that moment. The silence contains a lot of messages:

"I think I am supposed to have memorized the way to do this."
"What could she possibly mean by 'another way?' "
"Wouldn't 'another way' be cheating or wrong?"
"I am not going to say anything and look foolish."
"I don't know how to think about this question."

At this point, Carole decides that the students need exposure to other methods of solving the problem in order to have something to talk about. In the days that follow, they review place value and the traditional subtraction algorithm in more concrete ways, using pictures or base-10 blocks. Then Carole reminds the students that some people never subtract! They count up from 129 to 132. This is the "counting-up" strategy. Once children realize the latitude they are given to initiate alternative methods (that make sense), the energy level in the class increases. When the class returns to the "regrouping" algorithm, they have a renewed understanding of what they are doing and have many insights to share. Soon, they clamor for the opportunity to come up to the front of the class to explain different ways to solve problems.

"Try Something": Assessing Risk-Taking Capacity
(First–Sixth Grade)

Another way we diagnose the class's readiness for risk taking is to pose a problem that requires thinking outside of familiar patterns. In some children's prior math experiences the teacher has demonstrated how to solve a problem, then students have practiced applying the same solution pattern over and over. There is not much thinking to explain. Children perceive themselves somewhere on a continuum of "getting it" or not. In order to have something to say about their thinking in solving a problem, children must have some real thinking to talk about!

A "guess-and-check" problem is ideal for assessment at the beginning of the year because it requires students to take an important first step in problem solving: *try* something! Most third graders at the start of the year know a procedure for solving a problem such as:

> Bob had 41 cookies in all. 17 are oatmeal cookies. The rest are chocolate chip. How many are chocolate chip cookies? (41 = 17 + ____ cookies.)

Consider adding another step to the problem:

> Bob had 41 cookies. He has 7 more chocolate chip than oatmeal. How many of each cookie could he have?"

This problem is harder! If students have previously experienced using a procedure for finding different combinations by guess and check, they might do something like the following:

> First try: 8 chocolate chip and 1 oatmeal
>
> (8 + 1 = 9 cookies: not enough cookies)
>
> Second try: 28 chocolate chip and 21 oatmeal
>
> (28 + 21 = 49 cookies: too many cookies)
>
> Third try: 24 chocolate chip and 17 oatmeal
>
> (24 + 17 = 41 cookies)

If students have not previously used a guess and check procedure, then they will have to come up with the idea on their own. We watch carefully. Do they freeze? Argue? Get frustrated? Does someone think of *trying something*? If so, does he or she share the idea? Do more and more children catch on and begin to figure it out together? Do they devise a table or list or another way of organizing their trials? At the beginning of the year students are usually near the "freezing" end of this spectrum. In many classes children need to be taught to *try something*. Once they do that, they can work alone or, better yet, collaborate to figure out how to adjust and get closer to a solution. These steps involve risk taking! We begin to model and teach problem solving and risk taking through discussions in whole-group lessons and we guide children as they practice in partnerships and small groups.

Encouraging math talk between students and framing lessons around students' conversation is a major change from the traditional teacher-driven math lesson where they are only called upon to answer the teacher's question. We believe math discussion deepens students' understanding of math concepts and we think it is well worth the effort to include it in daily lessons.

Math Wizard (First–Fifth Grade)

In the primary grades, especially, risk taking can happen just because the activity is fun. An approach for promoting discussion among younger children is to have a "math wizard" of the day who designs a problem and shares his or her solution with the class. After the wizard shares, other students may share their solutions or ask questions of the wizard. The wizard wears a specially designed hat or holds a wand to designate the job. Since most children enjoy a dynamic presentation, the teacher can get a lot of mileage out of relatively simple costumes or props.

Thought-Provoking Open Questions (K–Sixth Grade)

Open questions—questions that cannot be answered in one or two words—invite math-talk participation by all students. For example, the teacher may present a general concept in the form of a question: "How do people use fractions?" When the teacher elicits ideas from all students and records them on a chart that remains up for a time, she or he promotes a message that everyone's thoughts are very important to the class.

Open questions can also be used to highlight an important word. Select a word and ask for any connections. The teacher can record them on a word web. A *word web* is a circle with a target word in the center. Spokes coming out from the center circle are used to jot related words down and to visually connect them to the target word. For example, using the word *calendar*, a lesson can begin by asking "What is a calendar?" This may be followed by answers or further questions that lead to what a calendar is used for and to a discussion of other types of measurement. After making connections, students may categorize the words based on the identified purposed for a calendar.

A computation problem such as _____ = 9 + 8 may invite a discussion about the equal sign, the reversed number sentence format, and doubles plus one. An opening question such as, "Do you notice anything different?" followed by "Why is the equal sign first?" and "Does the placement in front change anything?" helps to get the talk going. As another example, problem solving about how four students share 14 pennies may lead to a discussion involving arrays, division, and remainders.

Once students have begun to think about the problem, the teacher often extends the beginning talk using follow-up questions. These questions help to get more students involved. Questions such as, "Does anyone have another way?" "Who agrees or disagrees and why?" or "Who wants to add to this idea?" prompt more students to respond and serve as models for student-driven discussions in the future. The teacher encourages as many students as possible to contribute and begins to construct an environment where the conversation is among students.

In Patti's second grade, some children would repeat the same thoughts as their friends just to be heard. As the children became comfortable with discussing open questions, some began to say such things as, "I agree with Jon." Eventually, they began to give credit to another student. When Tyler said, "Andrea really thought of that," Patti knew that not only was Tyler listening to others, but he was realizing that the process was more important than being the one who thought of a particular idea.

Teacher Think-Alouds (K–Sixth Grade)

Students must understand a problem clearly in order to be prepared for the risk taking involved in problem solving. Therefore, a teacher "think-aloud" is a helpful scaffold for introducing a problem and setting up math talk. The teacher may read the problem twice; once quickly, and once to vocalize her or his thinking about the vocabulary, the information, and the question in the problem. The teacher also thinks aloud to model how to solve the problem. What operation should be used? Should I draw a picture? Should I guess and check or make an estimate? Does the answer make sense? Am I answering the question asked in the problem?

While experimenting with ways to help students get better at using their reflective abilities for reading, Ogle (1992) noticed charts in classrooms listing steps for solving math problems. She found that many students could successfully transfer the math problem-solving steps to their thinking about the stories they were reading. Ogle reports that both teachers and students were surprised to make this connection between math and literature, but once they noticed it, they readily applied it.

Ogle (1992, p. 30) writes, "Many students have found this new *stance* as a reader–problem solver energizing and motivating." In the discussions that followed, the teachers in Ogle's study stated that "the students [were] thinking deeply." It is helpful for students when we make connections like these directly in our think-alouds. We find that students who are invited explicitly to apply their problem-solving strengths for reading to their thinking in math, and vice versa, become more confident risk takers in both areas.

Teachers can also look for opportunities to model thinking, such as "Where did I get stuck in this problem?" This helps students think of math as a process with steps and procedures. Students begin to realize that, even if they have not completed the task, they have understood and solved some parts of the problem. They know more than they thought they did! Students who are advanced math thinkers often volunteer that they have erred and articulate what they were confused about. When teachers value and model the same articulation, they reinforce this kind of reflection.

Preteaching to Support Quieter Voices (K–Fourth Grade)

Supporting the voices of the quieter children is crucial to creating a talking culture. Sometimes in the beginning of the year only a few children speak. Many appear to lack confidence that they have anything to add to a conversation. The perception can be that a few talkative "smart" children are the only ones expected to talk. To address this, we continually give the message that everyone will be heard, then find ways to *make sure that everyone's contributions are needed.*

How do we do this? Sometimes it is nothing more than giving the class "think time." The class begins to understand that we will ask questions of everyone, and that we will give time for thinking before speaking. Then we make sure to ask questions that are crafted with a particular child in mind. We use what we have observed about a specific child's understandings from conferencing or other guided small-group work. We identify places in the lesson where we can ask questions that draw on that child's knowledge and call on him or her in the whole-class lesson when that knowledge is needed. The class, expecting to hear the more vocal and confident children, begins to hear new voices making contributions that help everyone's thinking. Slowly the culture of talk shifts toward including the entire class.

As classroom teachers who teach reading, we know a lot about the power of building background knowledge. We preteach vocabulary before children read as a way of helping all students approach a passage with more equal background knowledge. Similarly, in math, we often preteach a problem-solving strategy to one or two children. That prior knowledge helps them understand the lesson and gives them the power to contribute to the discussion.

Teacher Coaching for Small Group Problem Solving Using Manipulatives (K–Sixth Grade)

When we know the class needs support in working together to solve problems, we look for questions and prompts to encourage them.

"How can you work together to get this job done in the short time you have?"
"How can you divide up the work?"
"Trust your partner—you only have so much time to finish."

Early one year Barbara Hiller worked with a group of third graders to sort and count base-10 blocks (blocks with values of 1, 10, or 100, depending on their size). Working together to count the blocks caused a group breakdown. Barb observed this and encouraged them with questions like those above. Additional questions that guided the children to successful completion were:

"Can you estimate about how many blocks you think you have?"
"How might you use this place-value chart to sort the blocks?"
"How could that help you estimate?"

We have found it is easier for children to problem solve together when they start with concrete problems. Because this group was working with blocks, they could see in a concrete way how to divide them up for counting when the teacher suggested it. Tangrams, snap-cubes, pattern blocks, jigsaw puzzles, and attribute block puzzles all provided further opportunities for shared problem solving in this class. After that, they were able to move to solving more abstract problems cooperatively.

Anchor Charts (K–Sixth Grade)

As mentioned in the last chapter, we use anchor charts routinely in our language-rich math classrooms. These charts, handwritten on poster paper, record the class's shared thoughts over time. We put them together through class discussion, hang them in the room and return to them to discuss and analyze how the class has improved. Sometimes we refer to a chart at the beginning of a cooperative working or talking session to identify one aspect to work on. Some examples of topics for charts are:

➢ Why we need to have math conversations.

➢ What we did well together today.

➢ Setbacks—solving problems with talking and working together.

➢ Suggestions for talking and working together more productively. "If you could ask your classmates to do one thing better tomorrow, what would it be?"

In the following example, Patti developed an anchor chart with her second graders on how to solve problems. The particular lesson involved solving a multistep problem. Patti prepared her class by asking students to think about *how* they go about solving the problem.

"Today's lesson will not only be on solving the problem but also on what are the steps we use to solve most problems? Let's work through this problem together."

After she read the problem aloud, Patti asked a student, "What is the problem about? Can you retell the problem in your own words?" Patti wrote the retelling under the original problem. Then, making use of a think-aloud, she suggested that a picture or drawing of the problem might be helpful. She asked if anyone was comfortable drawing a picture on the board. Of course, she had a volunteer. Next,

---

What to Do to Solve a Problem

1. Read the problem and then retell it in your own words.
2. Find important words in the story.
3. Draw a picture or diagram of the problem.
4. Solve the problem.
5. Write a number model.
6. Explain how and why you came to the solution.

FIGURE 2.3. Anchor chart for problem solving (second grade).

the class discussed different strategies to solve the problem. As Patti observed her students, she realized that they were very good at discussing strategies. However, they were less secure in finding math words. The obvious ones, such as "how much" or "add" were quickly identified. Selecting "ordinary" words or phrases with special math meanings was much more difficult for them.

Once they all agreed on a strategy and in this case, a number sentence, Patti asked a student to explain the solution and justify the answer with the given details of the story. After walking through this problem-solving experience, Patti reviewed the steps with the class and wrote the anchor chart shown in Figure 2.3 to support the process.

Paper Bag Problems: Introducing Unfamiliar Problems (Second–Sixth Grade)

Sometimes we give problems to children in paper bags instead of on sheets of paper, just for fun. We also use this approach as a way to introduce children to unfamiliar problems. We may start with a familiar pattern and then carefully and gradually choose less familiar problems that extend and vary the pattern. This leads children to more resourceful and creative thinking.

For example, the teacher writes several problems with a similar pattern on a page, cuts them apart, and puts them in paper bags (Van de Walle, 2003). Children enjoy pulling a problem out of the bag, solving it, and drawing or writing about their procedure. For example:

> Maureen brought 185 colors of crayons for the class to try. On the first day, 36 of them were tried. How many crayons are left to try?

(185 − 86 = 99 crayons)

Children can practice with the teacher's guidance in math class, then independently as part of center time.

Gradually problems with a second step are added. For example:

> Maggie brought 185 colors of crayons for the class to try. In the first week the children had used 86 of the colors. In the second week, they used 14 more colors. How many crayons were still left to try?

$(185 - 86 = 99)$ and then $(99 - 14 = 85)$ crayons

Or

$185 - (14 + 86) = 85$ crayons

Eventually open-ended problems are included. For example:

> Make up a problem to go with $185 - 86$. Show how you solved the problem. Use words, numbers, or pictures to show your thinking.

The teacher leads a discussion where children share their thinking about some of the problems. When the class is ready to talk about their thinking, the teacher invites children to go to the board to show and explain some of their problem-solving processes. The familiarity they developed with the gradually varied problems enables them to engage in a dialogue in which children ask each other to justify their thinking. They begin to put themselves in someone else's problem-solving mind and to look with interest when someone becomes "stuck." They begin to see that following an erroneous path looking for a solution can be a lot better than no path at all, and that much can be learned by exploring a mistake and talking about ways to adjust.

Discussing Mathematical Conjectures (K–Sixth Grade)

It is standard procedure for mathematicians to make assertions, or conjectures, which they and others then try to prove or disprove. Once the conjecture is agreed upon it becomes a theorem (Ball & Bass, 2001). It is fun to practice justifying mathematical ideas by discussing children's mathematical conjectures. In Carole's third-grade class, a *conjecture* is a mathematical idea proposed by her or someone in the class. The person who proposes the idea posts it on the bulletin board and presents it to the class. The idea is then open for discussion. As long as there is anyone who doubts, asks for further clarification, or proposes a scenario where it might not be true, the idea remains a conjecture. Students are invited to discuss, raise questions, and defend their opinions. Once everyone is convinced that the proposal is true, it can be posted as a *theorem*. One year a student wrote a conjecture.

> STEPHEN: I think that every time a number is multiplied by 10, every number is moved up one digit and a zero is put in the 1's place. [conjecture]

CAROLE: Can we put that up on the wall as a *theorem* we all agree on? Can anyone think of a time when that might not be true?

ANGELA: Well, what if it might not work for negative numbers?

STEPHEN: Hmm . . . well, let me work on that . . .

The dialogue went on for weeks. Whenever the children almost agreed, someone would raise doubt and would need to be convinced again. Those who had taken a position would argue it over and over, finding various numbers to "prove" their case. When the class began to study decimals and fractions the conjecture had to be adjusted, again providing ample opportunities for children to work on developing mathematical reasoning through discussion. Stephen's conjecture continually provided a point of reference for the class. When a problem came up that required multiplying a number by 1,000, the teacher was able to remind the students, "Well, you will need Stephen's conjecture to solve that problem."

The activities in this chapter are used to start children talking about math. In the next chapter, we look at how to help math talk get better and take off.

CHAPTER 3

HELPING CHILDREN GET BETTER AT MATH TALK

I n this chapter we examine what goes on in the classroom as math talk gets better, and a "community of discourse" takes shape. We consider daily lessons where students expect to make sense, to talk and listen to each other, to have problem-solving strategies, and to explain them. When students talk through problems together, the discussions get longer and children begin to manage cooperative groups more independently.

WHAT HAPPENS WHEN MATH TALK GETS BETTER

We know the classroom talk is getting better when students and the teacher see it as the backbone of daily math classes. You know it is really progressing when the hands go up immediately, as more and more children become eager to contribute to the class discussion.

Hufferd-Ackles et al. (2004) provide a framework for the development of math-talk learning communities. Consisting of a progression through four (0 to 3) levels each for teachers and students, the framework outlines a shift from a focus on answers with the teacher as leader to a focus on mathematical thinking with the teacher as coach and assister. As shown in Table 3.1, the framework informs our evaluation of students' competencies and our decisions about how to support their growth. More specifically, we look for progress as indicated by these student behaviors:

➢ A focus on thinking rather than just answers

➢ Listening in order to understand one another

➢ Paraphrasing each other's explanations

➢ Expecting their explanations to make sense

➢ Seeing errors as opportunities for learning

➢ Using explanations about a problem as a stimulus for whole-group talk

➢ Understanding that their ideas will give rise to the content of some lessons

As the math talk gets better, students are eager to explore and are not anxious about needing the right answer in a very short time. They expect explanations to make sense. The teacher encourages children to question one another.

"Does it make sense? Jeremy, did it make sense to you, what Jonah just said? Not really? Jonah, could you explain again? Could you come up here and show us on the board?"

Another characteristic of a class that is becoming comfortable and secure is that students begin to admit or see their mistakes and want to explain where their thinking went wrong. It is quite admirable for students to wish to share, putting their egos aside.

JEREMY: (*Regarding another problem*) Oh, I thought it was two dimensional, not three dimensional.

JEREMY: (*on another day*) I couldn't decide whether to add the first two numbers or all three.

Jeremy's interjections reveal the ability to reflect and correct his thinking. They give the teacher an opportunity to show that student errors are opportunities for learning. The class begins to see that errors can lead to interesting discussions that help everyone learn.

Sometimes student explanations about a problem expand to a long whole-group talk. When Carole introduced multidigit multiplication to her third-grade class, the opening problem of the day turned into a two-day talk. Carole wanted to begin with children's invented algorithms, so she got them started by asking them to work on their own to come up with ways to find out "How much are eight 300s?" She walked around the room admiring their inventiveness as they tried out their ideas. Then she asked them to share.

TEACHER: Corinne, would you please put your solution on the board for us? (*Shows four groups of 300 + 300 = 600, for a total of 2,400.*) Does anyone have a different way? (*Calls on Ella, who writes her solution on the board.*)

ELLA: (*Begins by adding 8 + 8 + 8 = 24.*) Three eights equal 24. If you do that 10 times, you have 30 eights. You get 10 twenty-fours. That is 240. Thirty

TABLE 3.1. Levels of the Math-Talk Learning Community: Action Trajectories for Teacher and Student

A. Questioning	B. Explaining mathematical thinking	C. Source of mathematical ideas	D. Responsibility for learning
Overview of shift over Levels 0–3:			
The classroom community grows to support students acting in central or leading roles and shifts from a focus on answers to a focus on mathematical thinking.			
Shift from teacher as questioner to students and teacher as questioners.	Students increasingly explain and articulate their math ideas.	Shift from teacher as the source of all math ideas to students' ideas also influencing direction of lesson.	Students increasingly take responsibility for learning and evaluation of others and self. Math sense becomes the criterion for evaluation.
Level 0: Traditional teacher-directed classroom with brief answer responses from students.			
Teacher is the only questioner. Short frequent questions function to keep students listening and paying attention to the teacher.	*No or minimal teacher elicitation of student thinking, strategies, or explanations; teacher expects answer-focused responses. Teacher may tell answers.*	*Teacher is physically at the board, usually chalk in hand, telling and showing students how to do math.*	*Teacher repeats student responses (originally directed to her or him) for the class. Teacher responds to students' answers by verifying the correct answer or showing the correct method.*
Students give short answers and respond to the teacher only. No student-to-student math talk.	No student thinking or strategy-focused explanation of work. Only answers are given.	Students respond to math presented by the teacher. They do not offer their own math ideas.	Students are passive listeners; they attempt to imitate the teacher and do not take responsibility for the learning of their peers or themselves.
Level 1: Teacher beginning to pursue student mathematical thinking. Teacher plays central role in the math-talk community.			
Teacher questions begin to focus on student thinking and focus less on answers. Teacher begins to ask follow-up questions about student methods and answers. Teacher is still the only questioner.	*Teacher probes student thinking somewhat. One or two strategies may be elicited. Teacher may fill in explanations him- or herself.*	*Teacher is still the main source of ideas, though she or he elicits some student ideas. Teacher does some probing to access student ideas.*	*Teacher begins to set up structures to facilitate student listening to and helping other students. The teacher alone gives feedback.*
As a student answers a question, other students listen passively or wait for their turn.	Students give information about their math thinking usually as it is probed by the teacher (minimal volunteering of thoughts). They provide *brief descriptions* of their thinking.	Some student ideas are raised in discussions, but are not explored.	Students become more engaged by repeating what other students say or by helping another student at the teacher's request. This helping mostly involves students showing how they solved a problem.

Level 2: Teacher modeling and helping students build new roles.

Some co-teaching and co-learning begins as student-to-student talk increases. Teacher physically begins to move to side or back of the room.

Teacher continues to ask probing questions and also asks more open questions. She or he also facilitates student-to-student talk (e.g., by asking students to be prepared to ask questions about other students' work).

Students ask questions of one another's work on the board, often at the prompting of the teacher. Students listen to one another so they do not repeat questions.

Teacher probes more deeply to learn about student thinking and supports detailed descriptions from students. Teacher open to and elicits multiple strategies.

Students usually give information as it is probed by the teacher with some volunteering of thoughts. They begin to take a position and articulate more information in response to probes. They explain steps in their thinking by providing fuller descriptions and begin to defend their answers and methods. Other students listen supportively.

Teacher follows up on explanations and builds on them by asking students to compare and contrast them. Teacher is comfortable using student errors as opportunities for learning.

Students exhibit confidence about their ideas and share their own thinking and strategies even if they are different from others. Student ideas sometimes guide the direction of the math lesson.

Teacher encourages student responsibility for understanding the mathematical ideas of others. Teacher asks other students questions about student work and whether they agree or disagree and why.

Students begin to listen to understand one another. When the teacher requests, they explain other students' ideas in their own words. Helping involves clarifying other students' ideas for themselves and others. Students imitate and model teacher's probing in pair work and in whole-class discussions.

Level 3: Teacher as co-teacher and co-learner.

Teacher monitors all that occurs, still fully engaged. Teacher is ready to assist, but now in more peripheral and monitoring role (coach and assister).

Teacher expects students to ask one another questions about their work. The teacher's questions still may guide the discourse.

Student-to-student talk is student-initiated, not dependent on the teacher. Students ask questions and listen to responses. Many questions are "Why?" questions that require justification from the person answering. Students repeat their own or other's questions until satisfied with answers.

Teacher follows along closely to student descriptions of their thinking, encouraging students to make their explanations more complete; may ask probing questions to make explanations more complete. Teacher stimulates students to think more deeply about strategies.

Students describe more complete strategies; they defend and justify their answers with little prompting from the teacher. Students realize that they will be asked questions from other students when they finish, so they are motivated and careful to be thorough. Other students support with active listening.

Teacher allows for interruptions from students during explanations; she or he lets students explain and "own" new strategies. (Teacher is still engaged and deciding what is important to continue exploring.) Teacher uses student ideas and methods as the basis for lessons or mini-extensions.

Students interject their ideas as the teacher or other students are teaching, confident that their ideas are valued. Students spontaneously compare and contrast and build on ideas. Student ideas form part of the content of many math lessons.

The teacher expects students to be responsible for co-evaluation of everyone's work and thinking. She or he supports students as they help one another sort out misconceptions. The teacher helps and/or follows up when needed.

Students listen to understand, then initiate clarifying other students' work and ideas for themselves and for others during whole-class discussions as well as in small-group and pair work. Students assist each other in understanding and correcting errors.

Note. From Hufford-Ackles, Fuson, and Sherin (2005). Copyright 2005 by the National Council of Teachers of Mathematics. Reprinted by permission.

49

eights is 240. If you do 10 of those, you have 300 eights. That equals 2,400, because 10 two hundred forties equal 2,400.

(Note: The teacher makes a decision to accept Ella's application of the commutative property of multiplication here. She briefly checks with the class and sees that they seem to accept that 3 eights will be the same as 8 threes—or, looking ahead, that 300 eights will be the same as 8 three hundreds. The children have already worked with this concept using single-digit multiplication facts.)

Because the class was so engaged, the teacher continued asking various children to share their solutions. Many students were amazed that the answer kept coming out the same, no matter what procedure was followed. In a few more minutes the chalkboard was covered with different ways to do the same computation, and many students had the chance to explain their thinking to the class.

This process takes longer than just telling the class how to do the computation. But it can be appropriate for some lessons. By the time a formal algorithm for multidigit multiplication is introduced in Carole's class, the children have had a chance to try their own ideas. They have a thorough understanding of the quantities involved in the problem and how they change as they are multiplied. Sometimes one of the student examples, such as Ella's, is actually very close to the algorithm to be taught. As a result, the content of a planned lesson can seem to be derived from student ideas.

"Look. Ella added 3 eights and got 24. She said, 'If 3 eights are 24, then 30 eights are 240 because you have 10 groups of 3 eights. Then 300 eights are 2,400 because you have 10 groups of 30 eights.' Here is a way to write that":

$$3 \times 8 = 24$$
$$30 \times 8 = 240$$
$$300 \times 8 = 2,400$$

or

$$\begin{array}{r} 300 \\ \times\ 8 \\ \hline 2,400 \end{array}$$

Using the Levels of the Math-Talk Learning Community framework, we see that this class is functioning nicely in Level 2: The teacher moves to the back of the room as "students exhibit confidence about their ideas and share their own thinking and strategies even if they are different from others. Student ideas sometimes guide the direction of the math lesson" (Hufferd-Ackles et al., 2004). This is one of the ways it looks as the discussions get better.

STRATEGIES FOR STUDENT-LED CONVERSATIONS

Teachers who support children's problem solving provide frequent opportunities for them to collaborate in partnerships and small groups. As children's confidence increases for approaching new problems, for making sense of mathematics, and for talking productively, their problem-solving discussions become more complex and independent. We noticed that our students were transferring skills from their literature discussion groups quite readily to math discussions, so we began using similar structures to support math talk in groups. The following presents some ways we have found to scaffold independence for mathematical conversations. These include the creation and use of a set of explicit rules, or a rubric, for small-group discussions, math conversations based on a planned set of interactions, and math conversations with assigned roles. In each of these cases, consideration should be given to the composition of the group.

Selecting Groups

Some children begin talking and risk taking more easily in partnerships and then can move to groups of three and then four. Factors we consider in forming groups of children are:

➢ How to meet the needs of various students. Children of differing mathematics abilities may complement each other in a group as one person may need to practice articulating his or her thinking steps while others need to hear the explanation.

➢ How students will move from a partnership to a group setting. As teachers, we reflect on who can work well together and who needs to be separated. However, as the math community in the classroom develops, students will discover each other's strengths and learn how to work productively with everyone in the class.

➢ How to create flexible groups. Students should have the opportunity to interact with all students in the class in the course of a school year. As students develop skills for working collaboratively, we plan new groupings that support their needs and offer new challenges. Sometimes we group students of like readiness to challenge their thinking, and sometimes we group students heterogeneously to stretch their ability to teach and learn from each other.

Creating and Using a Rubric for Small-Group Discussions

To support children in conducting small-group discussions independently, Carole worked with them to define successful behaviors. After several months' thinking, one class created the Mathematical Conversation Rubric shown in Figure 3.1. This chart lists the types of behavior needed by each child to make a group discussion

	3	2	1
Materials	I help the group make sure everyone has all the right materials before starting.	I only help some people to get the right materials.	I get only my materials, and start before the rest of the group is set up.
Understanding what to do	I read the directions or problem carefully. I work with others to figure out the directions or problem and make sure everyone understands before we begin.	I help a little bit to make sure everyone understands the directions or problem.	I start by myself before everyone understands the directions or problem.
Focus	I stay focused on talking about the problem or game.	I talk mostly about the problem or game.	I talk about topics not related to the problem or game.
Sharing strategies	I say my ideas to the group. I help make sure everybody has a chance to try out their ideas to see if they work.	I try a little bit to give the group ideas.	I do not talk about my ideas.
Listening	I listen to others and am able to paraphrase what they say. I agree, add on, or question their ideas.	I build on others' ideas a little bit. Sometimes I forget to paraphrase what they say.	I get stuck on my own ideas and do not listen to others.
Taking turns	I give everyone a chance to think, and then ask what they are thinking.	I sometimes remember to ask what others are thinking.	I do not find out what others are thinking.
Cleaning up	I stick with the group until everything is cleaned up.	I help clean up, but I leave the group before the clean-up is completed.	I do not help clean up.

FIGURE 3.1. Mathematical conversation rubric.

successful, and it explicitly describes what those behaviors look like when done very well (3 points), medium well (2 points), and poorly (1 point). There was a heated discussion among the students about whether the ranking columns should be labeled "3–2–1," or "2–1–0." After describing the lowest benchmarks, ("I get only my materials, and start before the rest of the group is set up," etc.) the children decided that those undesirable behaviors should be worth "0" points! Another teacher, hearing about the debate, thought there might be some situations where students would need to get one point for those behaviors in order to get credit for starting! This is the kind of discussion that can be expected when students participate in the creation of such a rubric.

Before each small-group talk the children knew which benchmark they would be working on that day. Carole noted their successes as she circulated among the groups and shared them during the discussion afterward.

A Planned Mathematical Problem-Solving Conversation

In an example of the significance of "good" questions, Sullivan (1991, p. 130) describes a student who could successfully calculate perimeter and area when the task followed a familiar pattern, where diagrams of rectangles were shown with their dimensions. But when the question was, "A rectangle has a perimeter of 30 units. What might be its area?" the student was unable to understand the problem. Even after clarifying possible difficulties with the language of the question, Sullivan concluded that the student "had learned to answer routine exercises but had not fully understood the concepts." In our experience, a good question for discussion challenges children to consider more than one possible answer, or more than one possible approach to the solution.

For the mathematics conversation described below, Carole chose a problem for which the students had not been shown similar examples. A fairly wide variety of approaches might have been used to solve it given the knowledge and previous experiences she knew the class had.

Carole began by planning the sequence of interactions. There are always time constraints, and she had a total of 30 to 40 minutes for the entire discussion lesson. The planned sequence of interactions and their time allotments are summarized in Figure 3.2. The following describes how the lesson unfolded.

Introduce the Problem or Prompt to the Whole Class (5 Minutes)

Carole gathers the children together to read the problem. She gives them time to read it silently. Then the class takes a few minutes to read and clarify together. She reminds them that the first step is to make sure to understand the problem.

> There are 5 chocolate bars. They each come with marks showing 6 equal sections. Eight people want to share the 5 chocolate bars. How can they do it? (Origin of this problem is unknown.)

> 1. Introduce the problem or prompt to the whole class (5 minutes)
> 2. Students begin working on the problem individually (5 minutes)
> 3. Students collaborate in small groups or with partners (10–15 minutes)
> 4. Whole-group discussion (5–20 minutes, or longer if there is time)
> 5. Whole-group instruction (next day)

FIGURE 3.2. Plan for a mathematical conversation.

Students Begin Working Individually on the Problem (5 Minutes)

Carole says, "I will give you a few minutes to get started on your own. Then work with your partners." Taking a few minutes for individual work is an important step in this process. It gives responsibility to each child for trying the problem. Without this step, some students wait until the group meets and then rely solely on others for their thinking, without contributing any thoughts of their own. Children appreciate having time to think and work alone before beginning to collaborate. It is not essential for them to have enough time to work all the way through the problem, but they should be able to get a start.

It is also important to emphasize to the children that sharing their thinking about the *process* is really the important part of the lesson. Carole says, "I do not expect you necessarily to finish solving it. But I expect you to try something, and then to explain to the class how far you have gotten."

Students Collaborate in Small Groups or with Partners (10–15 minutes)

Children work together to solve the problem. During this time the teacher circulates, watching and listening, looking for similarities or differences in the ways the groups are thinking and working. It is helpful to take notes in order to share specific observations about the interactions or content of the talk when the class comes back together.

Eleanor and Laura are able to problem solve together at points where they get "stuck," and eventually reach a solution.

> ELEANOR: (*Trying different ways of drawing a distribution of 5 chocolate bars with 6 pieces each among 8 people*) So . . . we both have the same idea.
>
> LAURA: I am going to count them up again.
>
> ELEANOR: This is not split equally. I only got 3 for person number 7.
>
> LAURA: What did you end with? I think mine is different.
>
> ELEANOR: I am going to try a different way. . . . Bingo! . . . Wait . . . How many little things are there? Do you know what 30 divided by 8 is? Divide by 8.

> Authors' note: (30 ÷ 8 = 3, with a remainder of 6, or 3 and ¾)

LAURA: I'm going to try it a little different from you.

ELEANOR: It never works! I have tried it twice.

LAURA: It is even. Each person gets 4 parts. Trust me.

ELEANOR: I am not going to trust you until I can do it for myself.

LAURA: We can divide this up to 8. . . . See?

ELEANOR: I am trying to color them all differently.

LAURA: Look, this is my way and I am going to show you. This is one right here. Why don't we just divide them up?

ELEANOR: Divide up the squares?
> Authors' note: (6 ÷ 8 = ¾)

LAURA: (*They both work on dividing up squares*) I did it! This one works! Each kid gets 4 plus a quarter of 1. . . . No . . .

BOTH: We solved it! 3¾ sections.
> Authors' note: (30 ÷ 8 = 3¾)

Looking at the Levels of the Math-Talk Learning Community framework in Table 3.1 (Hufferd-Ackles et al., 2004), we notice that Laura and Eleanor exhibit a Level 3 behavior: "Students spontaneously compare and contrast and build on ideas."

Whole-Group Discussion (5–20 Minutes, or Longer If There Is Time)

The teacher shares observations made during the small-group problem solving. Various groups then share their thinking and solutions for the problem in a whole-group math talk. This is a good place for the teacher to use the Levels of the Math-Talk Learning Community framework (Hufferd-Ackles et al., 2004) for guidance. The teacher needs to consider:

➢ How to help the class listen actively

➢ What to do when explainers get stuck

➢ What to do when explainers veer off in an irrelevant direction

➢ Observing students' thinking and using teacher's math knowledge to guide it

➢ Asking clarifying questions, making comparisons among strategies and providing a model by guiding children in probing others' thinking

For example, Carole starts by asking for students who were "stuck" to show their process. At this point in the year, there is enough trust in the group for children to be able to do this.

"I want somebody who is stuck but who can explain what you tried and where you are now."

While several children are writing on the board, Carole supports active listening by asking the rest of the students do two things: Look at the work that is unfolding, comparing it to their own; and write in their notebooks, either doing further work on their own solution, or try writing the steps in someone else's thinking as it is written on the board.

"Ooo, this is looking interesting. Look at what they are doing. Do some draw-ings in your notebook. Your job is to watch this right now and think, 'What are they thinking?' Emily, take a look. Do any of these look something like what you were doing? Look at that! Look at what Marion and Tyler drew!"

Children begin to share their thinking and Carole encourages the class to practice understanding someone else's process, putting themselves mentally in the other's place. She periodically asks them to paraphrase what has just been said.

"Who can explain what Gregg and Kenneth were saying and where they are stuck? Don't give them a clue yet about what else to try, but just . . . Who can explain what Gregg said?"

Soon the process becomes compelling. Students do listen and want to help each other figure things out. They begin to compare their strategies.

CHAD: (*Considering Maggie's strategy*) This is different.

JACKIE: I did the same thing.

MAGGIE: When we got here, we needed 2 more squares. We tried lots of dif-ferent ways, like giving 2 to each person, but that didn't work because we still needed 2 more squares . . . and then we tried 3, and then . . . it was time to stop.

CHAD: You guys were about to get it!

After several groups have explained, the teacher calls on Eleanor and Laura, who have reached a solution.

TEACHER: Eleanor, did you get all the way, or are you stuck?

ELEANOR: We got all the way, but we had, like, a thousand bad tries.

TEACHER: Oh good. That's a really important thing. One of the ways we learn the most is when we are stuck and then we try different things.

They begin their explanation by showing how they shaded various parts of their drawing. While this is an important part of their thinking, it appears lengthy, and Carole intends for this discussion to focus on understandings about fractions. So she steers them in that direction, hoping to minimize the representation issues for this day.

> TEACHER: So, tell what you were thinking next. Keep listening! Because they were stuck in basically the same place that the other 2 groups got stuck. . . . Now, this is how they worked their way out of it.
>
> ELEANOR: So then Laura had the genius idea that maybe we could split those in half! . . . or, in separate parts . . . 2.and then . . . she . . . I somehow thought well, maybe it would be 3. Somehow, I actually thought . . . I said, well, what if we divided it into 3s? This would be one, this would be one . . . and so on. That would be 10, though.
>
> JACKIE: I don't understand.
>
> ELEANOR: So, I decided, why don't I split up these 3 into smaller pieces? Then it would still be 9 people. So then I do a few more lines. (*She divides all 6 sections of the last chocolate bar in quarters.*) I already pretty much knew it was going to be 3. So then I put 1,1,1 on that one little section, 2,2,2 . . . 3,3,3 . . . 4,4,4 in this one, 5,5,5 in this one, 6,6,6 in this one, 7,7,7 in these, and 8,8,8 in these.
>
> TEACHER: So it came out even.
>
> ELEANOR: Yeah. They each get 3 pieces and ¾ of a piece.

In this exchange we see a math-talk community in action. Hufferd-Ackels et al. (2004, p. 83) refer to this as a process where "mathematical meanings are constructed through a process of interacting in a community."

> ELEANOR: (*Later*) "Mrs. Skalinder, you are absolutely right! I DID understand it better after I explained it with Laura!"

Whole-Group Instruction (Next Day)

In the final step of the sequence, the teacher has planned to make use of student understandings from the discussion to present the following day's lesson. The next day, Carole proceeded with the lesson from the math curriculum that introduces fractions. It went quickly, because she had already activated children's thinking and had gained detailed information about what they knew.

This is an example of what math talk looks and sounds like as it gets better. With continued support from the teacher, children begin to internalize the process. They become more and more independent about clarifying, questioning, and evaluating each other's thinking.

Math Discussions with Assigned Roles

One way to foster independence in math group discussions is for group members to have clearly defined responsibilities. This strategy is modeled on literature discussion groups with assigned roles (Daniels, 2002). Patti used this model with her second graders when she wanted the children to solve problems together in small groups without the teacher guiding the way. The class had already constructed an Anchor Chart for Problem Solving (see Figure 2.3) that could be used by the groups. Patti also wanted a way to help group members present their thinking to the class. She used the strategy of assigning roles.

Patti first selected a group of four students to learn and model the process. One student was given the responsibility of coordinator for the group. The coordinator was to make sure the steps on the anchor chart were followed and ensure that all members of the group took responsibilities that led to a presentation for the class. Everyone in the group was to read the problem and discuss its meaning in his or her own words. The coordinator then asked one person to write down the retelling of the problem on chart paper. Next each member of the group drew a diagram to support the story. After some discussion, the coordinator asked one student to draw the diagram on the chart paper. Of course this led to discussion about how to solve the problem. The possible strategies were discussed and the fourth student wrote how the group solved the problem and why they thought it worked. The model group worked through the problem and gave their presentation, explaining their solution and how to justify their thinking. Patti thought the class might be on their way to independence so she took the following steps a few days later.

She divided the whole class into groups, selecting one student from the model group to be in each new student group. She decided to give each group a different problem to solve. Other teachers might want the children to find different ways of solving the same problem. Patti passed out copies of the anchor chart for each child to follow in their group discussion. As the groups worked through the steps to solve their problems, the charts filled with information. Patti reminded the class to use their time wisely as she set the timer. A timer is a useful tool to remind children that their time together will end and that their work will be displayed.

It was difficult to get all of the presentations in during one class time so they were spread over a few days. This did not harm the presentations. Discussions such as these give the teacher flexibility to continue the work and talk when time allows.

Some helpful reminders include:

➢ Have a time limit set so everyone is reminded to keep working.

➢ If needed, assign numbers to each group member in the small groups to help the coordinator assign individual responsibilities.

➤ Remind students to help themselves understand the problem by looking at it in smaller "chunks."

➤ Review the terms or phrases used in the problem.

➤ Help children move the problem from abstract to concrete.

➤ Simplify the problem if needed: change to a one- or two-digit computation.

➤ Remind children to check that their strategy makes sense: estimate. Should the solution be smaller or larger than the numbers in the story?

➤ Remind each child to have their own paper or math journal available to work on the problem in their group.

➤ Chart paper or transparencies may be used for presentation.

During ensuing math discussions Patti noticed students who needed support for retelling the problem in their own words. To address retelling she returned to the "talking-and-listening sticks." Each pair of students took turns reading the problem while the other listened and then retold the problem in his or her own words.

Lisa followed a similar math conversation structure in her third-grade class by selecting a coordinator and assigning roles in small problem-solving groups. She added a template to involve all group members in reporting their solutions to the class. Lisa's Class Presentation Script can be found in Figure 3.3.

Coordinator: Good day! Before we present our math problem and solution, we will introduce our group members. (*Coordinator introduces group members.*) Now, _____ (*one of the group members*) will read and paraphrase the problem.

(***One group member*** reads the problem and then restates it.)

Coordinator: Now _____ (*another group member*) will present the important words from this problem.

(***Another group member*** presents a list of important words.)

Coordinator: _____ will explain our drawing.

(***Another group member*** presents the drawing.)

Coordinator: We saw that this problem could be solved by _____, so we _____.
We found out _____.

Coordinator: We will now take questions from the audience.

FIGURE 3.3. Class presentation script.

WHEN MATH TALK IS WORKING: AN INQUIRY PROJECT

When the mathematics talking community is rolling along, the teacher can conference with individuals and small groups because children know how to work productively and independently. They can help each other, where helping means that all parties benefit from the experience. Children solve problems cooperatively in small student-led groups. The teacher's job is to plan problems and tasks appropriate to students' needs.

Integrating math and literacy gives us opportunities to support the skills and knowledge students need for a shared inquiry project. In an inquiry, children are given time to explore their own methods for a given problem (e.g., find an algorithm for solving 84 − 67 = _____). Then they circulate and learn about the thinking of other "experts." They question each other, explain their methods, and learn new ways to look at and solve the problem. Finally, the whole class meets to share their thinking. They then make comparisons among the various methods and discuss which methods might work best for different types of problems. When we plan math inquiry projects, we follow the pacing and sequence of the math curriculum, but work on vocabulary, reading, writing, and talking skills with the aim of preparing students to sustain an in-depth inquiry into each other's computation or problem-solving methods.

Carole had her third-grade class undertake an inquiry for inventing and sharing subtraction algorithms. The project was planned as a culminating and synthesizing experience. The children would become resources for their classmates, sharing the expertise they had developed over time. To help organize the project, she used the inquiry framework shown in Figure 3.4. This framework is also applicable and adaptable for other major topics, such as data representation or any type of problem solving.

Prerequisites for Inquiry: Laying the Groundwork

For a successful inquiry, the teacher needs to have established a classroom community of active mathematics communication. This takes some time with every new group, even if students have had strong math literacy experiences in previous grades. Children need to be able to talk and listen to one another. They need the confidence to have their own strategies and the vocabulary to explain them. They need to be able to use manipulatives to model a problem for others and to represent their thinking with pictures, diagrams, and symbols. Options for scaffolding these skills are presented here and throughout the book.

The development of talking competency is especially important for the success of an inquiry project. In advance of the inquiry project Carole regularly identifies places in math lessons where she would invite children to:

Preparation
- Choose a big idea
- Plan for the activity to take place over several class periods
- Prepare one or two math problems
- Make a large Class Inquiry Chart
- Make individual student KWL Charts.

Stage 1. What I Know: Children Solve Problems Individually
- Children individually complete the "What I Know" column of their KWL Charts, describing a solution method for each math problem.

Stage 2. What I Want to Know: Children Learn of Alternate Methods from Class Experts
- Children briefly share their solutions with the whole class. Teachers lists different solution methods on the Class Inquiry Chart with names of their "experts."
- Children individually complete the "What I Want to Learn" column of their KWL Charts.

Stage 3. What I Learned: Children Teach Each Other
- Children move around the room to meet and learn other's methods, filling out the "What I Learned" section of their KWL Charts.
- As they learn new methods from the other "experts," children write them on slips of paper that they sign and post in the appropriate column on the Class Inquiry Chart.

Reflection. Apply Strategies to New Problems
- Whole-class application of methods to new problems.
- Discussion of which methods are best for various situations.

FIGURE 3.4. Framework for an inquiry project.

> Turn and talk with a partner
> Discuss with a small group and report back to the whole group
> Come to the board or overhead projector and explain their thinking to the class

Preparation for the Inquiry

In addition to choosing the topic for the inquiry, some advance planning and preparation of materials are necessary. First, one or two math problems should be selected as the basis for the inquiry. These problems should then appear on the following materials: one large Class Inquiry Chart and individual KWL Charts for each student.

Class Inquiry Chart

Using several yards of butcher paper, make one very large Class Inquiry Chart. Figure 3.5 shows the design with a row for each of the inquiry math problems and columns that will be used for noting various methods. Leave plenty of room for more columns, and add them as children invent more methods.

KWL Chart

Make KWL Charts and distribute to each student. KWL signifies "What We Know," "What We Want to Know," and "What We Learned" (Ogle, 1986). KWL is often used in a group setting; however, for purposes of the inquiry, Carole wanted to have a Class Inquiry Chart and each student to have their own KWL Chart. She altered the format to fit individual student use. Figure 3.6 shows the sheet for "What I Know" and "What I Want to Know." For the "What I Learned" section," Carole attached blank sheets of notebook paper for children to record their work on the problem. This provides the teacher with "tracks of their thinking" as they learn new strategies.

Appropriate Manipulatives

For the third stage of inquiry activities (see below) students will need to have appropriate tools available to help them explain their problem-solving methods to each other.

The Inquiry Activities

The full inquiry takes place in three stages.

Stage 1. What I Know: Children Solve Problems Individually

The KWL Charts are distributed. Each child then writes what he or she already knows in the "What I Know" (K) column showing their favorite method of computation for the problems. The teacher should circulate, observe, and possibly assist. This is the time where the teacher offers encouragement to students to stay with a method they are using, or quickly teach a new method to a very able student, or review a method using manipulatives with a student who needs extra support.

Stage 2. What I Want to Know: Children Learn of Alternate Methods from Class Experts

In this stage, children briefly share their solutions with the whole class, writing them on the chalkboard or on an overhead projector. The teacher lists each different strategy on the Class Inquiry Chart, along with the names of the experts who propose them. The teacher also writes the names of other children who wish to "sign on" as already expert for that method. After several strategies have been listed on the Class Inquiry Chart, children write in the KWL Chart's "What I Want to

What we learned	Method 1: Experts	Method 2: Experts	Method 3: Experts	Method 4: Experts	Method 5: Experts	Method 6: Experts	Method 7: Experts
Problem: (example:) 185 − 97							
Problem: (example:) 205 − 97							

FIGURE 3.5. Class inquiry chart.

From *Integrating Literacy and Math: Strategies for K–6 Teachers* by Ellen Fogelberg, Carole Skalinder, Patti Satz, Barbara Hiller, Lisa Bernstein, and Sandra Vitantonio. Copyright 2008 by The Guilford Press. Permission to photocopy this figure is granted to purchasers of this book for personal use only (see copyright page for details).

Name:	Word Problem:
Number Model:	
What I Know:	What I Want to Know from the Experts:

FIGURE 3.6. KWL chart (with just KW).

Learn" column. They list the names of the experts whose methods they would like to learn. To help motivate them, Carole tells her class that they are all required to know at least three methods. The class typically spends one period on the first and second stages where students propose various solution methods to the class.

Stage 3. What I Learned: Children Teach Each Other

The children sign up for a session with an expert. They move around the room and meet to learn each other's methods. They write on the notebook paper that is the "What I Learned" section attached to their KWL Charts. The teacher circulates and facilitates, usually taking notes about what various children are thinking. These observations may be used to bring students with similar lines of thought together. The teacher also reminds children that they are expert consultants and their job is to teach each other their strategies. The teacher advises the experts that one way to know for sure that the learner understands the new method is to have the learner explain it in their own words.

Children will need tools available to use as they are "teaching" each other. They may use base-10 blocks, number grids, and/or calculators to help them explain and demonstrate their thinking to one another. When the learners are confident with new strategies, they write a problem and solution on slips of paper and attach these to the Class Inquiry Chart in the proper column.

Reflection: Apply Strategies to New Problems

We use a class period or two to compare strategies in a whole-class discussion. The teacher presents some new problems and the class applies some of the learned strategies to these new problems. This leads to a discussion where students consider which computing methods are most efficient for particular situations.

In this example of an inquiry, we can tell students are talking effectively because they see themselves as resources for their classmates. These students have learned to be a mathematics community through supported growth that takes place over time.

CONCLUSION

Wanting a math-talk classroom and having a math-talk classroom are two different things. Often in more traditional mathematics classrooms, students just want to get the problem done or find the answer. Teachers feel rushed or pressured, so in many situations they read and explain the problem in their own words so the students can get back to plugging in the answers. We need to slow the process down purposely at times. Have students make predictions and talk about what needs to be done to solve a problem. Maybe it is just one student who is contributing at first, but that will change.

It helps for teachers to realize that it takes time for students to participate. Some are confident, while others are not comfortable with oral participation. It is essential to give them "think time" to think about what they want to say and allow others to process the information and respond. With patience, teachers can create a path to channel the "raw" resource of conversation into a constructive tool. The more modeling and encouragement students receive, the more comfortable they will become in sharing their thoughts and explaining their strategies. Not only will the whole class grow as a learning community, but partners will begin to have real conversations and small groups will function smoothly and come to consensus.

Many primary teachers have the luxury of being able to discuss a math problem or text in the reading or language arts block. Because primary teachers focus much of their instruction on reading, they often have many graphic organizers to aid in guided reading group discussions. Adding math content in reading blocks can be a big help to both students and teachers, not only in encouraging math talk but in overcoming some of the challenges presented by math texts. We turn to this area of math–literacy integration in the next chapter.

CHAPTER 4

ORIENTING CHILDREN TO MATH TEXTS

Doing math is more than just arithmetic; it also includes understanding and solving math problems, and reading and understanding the math book. This last task represents a great challenge for some of our students. In this chapter and the next, we present ideas and strategies for helping students to read math texts. These texts can include the student book, workbook or worksheets, supplemental materials, informational concept books, and even the problems placed on the board or overhead projector. We begin by explaining what it is that makes reading math text difficult for so many children. Understanding these challenges can help teachers know how to prepare students and then support them so they can successfully read the text.

MATH TEXTS: CHALLENGING READING

To read a math text with understanding, students need to know how it is organized and how it is similar to and different from other texts they read. Knowing that, they then need to know which reading strategies are most powerful for meeting their purposes. A number of factors frequently complicate student understanding. Some of these are intrinsic to math as a discipline, while others are posed by published math textbooks. The following are common challenges posed by math textbooks. Some of these can be addressed more easily than others.

➢ **Students are likely to encounter more math terms and concepts in earlier grades than was traditionally the case.** The content of mathematics lessons today is very different from the content many of us experienced years ago. Students are likely to encounter measurement, geometry, data, probability, and algebraic concepts as early as the primary grades. In the process of being exposed to more areas of mathematics, students encounter new and unfamiliar terminology. Our second-grade students are studying and learning about geometric shapes such as rectangular prisms and cylinders. In third grade, students are learning about solid figures such as cubes, dodecahedrons, and prisms, and how to take the first steps to visually solve a complex geometric problem. In fifth grade, our students are learning about applications of fractions to ratios. To understand terms such as prisms, area and perimeter, or fractions and ratios, students initially need to use their everyday language to describe these concepts. They can then learn the technical terms and begin to use them to communicate their ideas more precisely.

➢ **Some publishers provide many examples of real-world applications of the math concepts while others provide very few.** Students need many opportunities to explore and apply mathematical concepts to be facile in their use. They need to read about real-world examples, talk and write to demonstrate understanding, and draw to visualize problems. Teachers may need to supplement the main text with additional problems and possibly with informational texts on the same topic. For example, the text *Comparing Sizes and Weights* (Nguyen, 2006) may be used to more fully explore comparison, an important concept for solving many math problems.

➢ **Math and science texts contain more concepts per line, sentence, and paragraph than other kinds of texts** (Barton, Heidema, & Jordan, 2002). Math text is dense and often contains numerals and symbols in addition to words. Consider this example on reading decimals, from *Everyday Mathematics, Grade 4 Student Reference Book* (Bell et al., 2002a, p. 26).

> One way to read a decimal is to say it as you would a fraction. For example, 6.8 = 6 8/10, so 6.8 can be read as "six and eight-tenths." 0.001 = 1/1000 and is read as "one-thousandth." Sometimes decimals are read by first saying the whole number part, then saying "point," and finally saying the digits in the decimal part. For example, 6.8 can be read as "six point eight"; 0.15 can be read as "zero point one five." This way of reading decimals is often used when there are many digits in the decimal.

When planning lessons, teachers need an awareness of the concept and vocabulary load. They must also consider students' decoding skills and background knowledge. Students need many opportunities to observe teachers as they think aloud demonstrating how to make sense of the text before turning the task over to the students. We will come back to this idea later.

➢ **Math texts introduce new, technical vocabulary along with using familiar words in unfamiliar ways.** Kenney (2005, p. 3) explains why math vocabulary is difficult for many students: "Mathematics truly is a foreign language for most students: it is learned almost entirely at school and is not spoken at home. Mathematics is not a 'first' language; it does not originate as a spoken language, except for the naming of small whole numbers. Mathematics has both formal and informal expressions." Teachers can help students with the technical vocabulary through the use of metaphors. Whitin and Whitin (2000, p. 37) provide an example of students referring to composite numbers as King Kong numbers "because King Kong is big and the numbers are big." As suggested in Chapter 1, many teachers create math word walls and refer to them often, adding to the students' definitions as they learn more about the terms.

Teachers can also help students notice how the "little words" (e.g., *a*, *and*, *of*, *with*, *from*, etc.) have very specific meanings in math word problems. Later in this chapter we discuss how to help students understand words like *left*, *by*, and *each* in the context of solving math problems. Familiar words (e.g., *fact*, *multiple*, *similar*, *right*, *plane*, etc.) confuse students because they think they know the meaning of the word, but cannot figure out how it makes sense in the mathematical context. Teachers can support students by anticipating possible confusions. It can help to create an anchor chart with students of everyday words used differently in mathematics. Additional vocabulary issues will be addressed more fully in Chapter 6.

➢ **The placement of the main idea in math problems differs from that of the main idea in other texts** (Barton et al., 2002). In a math problem the main idea is typically found at the end of the paragraph rather than at the beginning and it is often in the form of a question. For example:

> A large cube is created out of many small white cubes of equal size. The large cube has 9 small cubes on each face. If you paint the outside of the large cube and then break apart the large cube into all of the small cubes, how many of the small cubes will *not* get paint on them? How many will have paint on one side? Two sides? Three sides?

In the above example, the main idea begins with the question, " . . . how many of the small cubes will *not* get paint on them?" Students need to know how information is presented within a problem in order to know what the problem is really about and how they might find a solution. Students can be helped to visualize problems with materials such as centimeter cubes and shown how to predict answers, a beginning step to solving a problem. Asking students to predict provides an entry into developing a plan for what initially appears very confusing.

Teachers can also help young students by pointing out the most important clue words such as *find*, *calculate*, *how many*, *much*, *more*, *what*, *which*, etc. It also helps to keep a running list of such words used to state the main idea.

➢ **Some students get lost in the details in the beginning of the math problem and cannot find the main idea. They may also have difficulty sorting out which details are important.**

The Fish House is a tiny restaurant. It has tables and seats for 21 people. It has the yummiest food in town. Six families are waiting to go in right now. There are 11 people in the Cook family and 12 people in the Bend family. There are only 7 Keys, but there are 10 Loops. There are 9 people in the Rush family, and there are 14 Traps. At the Fish House, all the people in a family eat at the same time. Which families can eat in the Fish House at the same time and fill all 21 seats? (from Hoogeboom & Goodnow, 1987, reprinted with permission)

In the above example, the authors are trying to account for the decoding ability of the students by using familiar words as the families' names. However, this is likely to add to students' confusion as they try to figure out what the Keys, Loops, and Traps have to do with the problem. Students are likely to have read these words in other contexts and have some definitional knowledge but that knowledge probably does not include use of the words as proper nouns. The students can get lost in all the confusing names and details. This is especially challenging for English language learners (ELLs).

➤ **Syntax in math problems is often unfamiliar.** Students are often confused by the word *each* as in, "There are five dogs in *each* of twenty pens . . . " or the phrase *times as much as*, as in "One amount is ten *times as much as* . . . " Teachers can help by explaining what such phrases mean just as they do when introducing students to unusual syntax in a reading lesson. Simple explanations, physical demonstrations, and repeated practice often provide enough support for students to understand the unusual word or phrase. However, it will take many exposures for students to figure out the meanings of unusual phrases before they do so independently. This is especially true for English language learners. It is important for teachers to be aware of possible confusions and to be prepared to address them.

➤ **Students are often introduced to the proper vocabulary terms before being allowed to use the concepts** (Whitin & Whitin, 2000). As an example, students are often introduced to the terms *area* and *perimeter* before having worked to understand what it means to measure an area or to discover what perimeter means. It is better to have students work with a concept before giving them the technical label. Talking, drawing, and writing their way to understanding, while working through engaging problems, allows students to explore concepts in concrete ways. Students learn to speak for themselves and soon come to realize that they need a label for describing what they are doing. At that point, the conventional term satisfies this need and supports their emerging understanding of the concept.

Not all of the above challenges are present in every math program. Some of the newer, standards-based math programs attempt to address these challenges. The textbooks in these programs "differ from traditional mathematics textbooks in that they present mathematical ideas in various contexts and engage students in exploring ideas, solving problems, sharing strategies, and building new knowledge based on solid conceptual understanding" (Reys, Reys, & Chavez, 2004, p. 65). These textbooks support teacher use of a workshop approach by recommending read-alouds to introduce or expand the understanding of concepts, suggest paired or group activities that encourage talk, and allow for sharing of ideas and thinking before, during, and at the end of the lesson. All of these activities increase the likelihood that students will engage meaningfully with the text.

Daniels and Zemelman (2004, p. 148) provide suggestions for helping students get the most out of their textbooks. While their audience is mostly middle and high school teachers, we have adapted their recommendations to apply to elementary teachers as well.

➢ Support children before they begin. Like Opitz and Ford (2001) and others, we recommend using lots of prereading activities to prepare students before asking them to read the text.

➢ Let children work together. Recognizing the power of collaboration, Daniels and Zemelman remind teachers to have students work together as they interact with the concepts and ideas presented in the text.

➢ Be selective and intentional when planning lessons (Daniels & Zemelman, 2004). Teachers must be selective in the language they use and in the elaborations they provide for particular lessons. As stated in the NCTM *Principles and Standards* (2000, p. 197), " . . . teachers must make on-the-spot decisions about which points of the mathematical conversation to pick up on and which to let go, and when to let students struggle with an issue and when to give direction." Some students may not be ready for in-depth discussions of concepts that they are just beginning to understand. While teachers have read the text many times, students are likely to be hearing it for the first time and, therefore, may experience quite a bit of confusion (Daniels & Zemelman, 2004). The important thing is to concentrate on building knowledge that all students need to understand the concepts. The teacher can then work with a small group that is ready for more elaboration if it seems appropriate.

The ideas that follow are based on the work of many researchers (Blachowicz & Ogle, 2001; Daniels & Zemelman, 2004; Draper, 2002; Vacca & Vacca, 1999) in the field of reading who suggest a before, during, and after framework as a model for demystifying the text and for engaging students as they grapple with the ideas presented in the text. We suggest "before" reading ideas to build background and to get students ready for the upcoming unit, "during" activities to help students persevere with new ideas presented in challenging reading, and "after" activities to help students consolidate the learning.

PREPARING STUDENTS TO READ MATH TEXT

Teachers are familiar with preteaching vocabulary and math terms. However, preteaching the terms may be premature. We prefer the more inclusive concept of frontloading to get students ready for a new mathematical learning. According to Opitz and Ford (2001), frontloading means activating students' prior knowledge about the concept, building background knowledge or providing additional background, assessing student strategy needs, increasing interest in the topic, and setting a purpose for reading. Specific strategies for introducing vocabulary are discussed in Chapter 6; we touch only on a few below.

Using Literature with Math Content as Read-Alouds

We use read-alouds as one way to frontload concepts for a new mathematics unit and to expose students to new vocabulary that they will encounter in the unit. After the books are read aloud by the teacher, they are placed in a prominent spot in the classroom and made available to students to reread during independent reading time. Blachowicz et al. (2006, p. 532) refer to this form of vocabulary development as incidental word learning. They continue by describing the benefits of reading aloud, especially for young children and, we believe, for ELL students. "Involving students in discussions during and after listening to a book has also produced significant word learning, especially when the teacher scaffolded this learning by asking questions, adding information, or prompting students to describe what they heard." This is exactly the kind of interactive read-aloud we promote in our classrooms.

Literature also provides a means for children to encounter mathematical concepts and vocabulary in the context of something familiar, a story. Several books (Bresser, 1995; Bamford & Kristo, 1998; Whitin & Whitin, 2000) and articles have suggested titles and sample lessons for including math read-alouds in the math class or workshop. In addition, many of the publishers of mathematics programs list literature titles for teachers to use in connection with particular units.

Laminack and Wadsworth (2006, p. 152) describe the advantages of using literature in all content areas: " . . . we believe that reading aloud from well-chosen picture books actually helps learners build the background understanding necessary to fully appreciate the information presented in most curriculum materials. In this way each read-aloud provides layers like the rings of an onion, one around the next. By the end of a unit of study learners are more grounded, having developed a more robust vocabulary with which to think about and discuss the topic. Learners have a pictorial repertoire to draw from as they try to envision the ideas being discussed. And they have a cache of stories to help them make sense of it all."

Deborah Shadle-Talbert (Shadle-Talbert, Rahn, & McMahon, 2000, p. 32), found that using children's literature produced a positive change in her first-grade students' attitude toward solving math problems. At the beginning of the year, 42%

of her students gave negative responses to the statement, "I like to solve math problems." By the end of the first semester, 86% of her students responded positively. Through read-alouds, Shadle-Talbert had exposed students to several books, some of which were directly related to the math concepts under study while others used story lines that she adapted for purposes of mathematical inquiry. Together, she and the children used the literature as the jumping-off point for posing problems that the characters might encounter where they would have to use their mathematical problem-solving skills to figure out a variety of situations that involved time and measurement, among other things.

Criteria for Selecting Books for Read-Alouds

Hunsader (2004, p. 618) states that, "Engagement with literature provides a natural way for students to connect the abstract language of mathematics to their personal world." She adapted a tool from Shiro (1997) for evaluating the literature and mathematics content of various books. Originally developed for picture books or storybook formats, we also found the criteria useful for evaluating the quality of informational math concept books that have an expository framework.

Hunsader's (2004, pp. 623–624) tool includes the following standards and suggests using a rating scale of 5 to 1, 5 being the highest.

Mathematics standards

➢ Is the book's mathematics content (text, computation, scale, vocabulary, and graphics) correct and accurate?

➢ Is the book's mathematics content visible and effectively presented?

➢ Is the book's mathematics content intellectually and developmentally appropriate for its audience?

➢ Do the book's mathematics and story complement each other?

➢ How great are the resources needed to help readers benefit from the book's mathematics?

Literary standards

➢ Does the plot exhibit good development, imagination, and continuity? Are the characters (if any) well developed?

➢ Does the book contain a vivid and interesting writing style that actively involves the child?

➢ Are the book's illustrations and graphics text-relevant, appealing, and representative of a child's perspective?

➢ Are the book's readability and interest level developmentally appropriate for the intended audience?

➤ Do the book's plot, style, and graphics/illustrations complement one another?

➤ Does the book respect the reader by presenting positive ethical and cultural values?

Hunsader studied and evaluated books found on the publishers' recommended read-aloud lists from several major mathematics textbook companies. She found great variability in the mathematical and literary quality of many of the recommended books. Therefore, she advises teachers to use an instrument like the above before deciding to include math-related storybooks in their math lessons. Without such an evaluation, precious time may be given to an activity with little instructional value. However, when the books are carefully chosen, they can motivate students and serve as a context for meaningful problem solving.

Making Read-Alouds Interactive

We recommend an interactive format for using read-alouds in math class. In an interactive format, the teacher first reads the book all the way through for the sheer enjoyment of it and to give students the gist of the story. Next, the teacher rereads the book, inviting the children into the reading by stopping at strategic points to ask questions, to think aloud about the math-related concepts, to make connections, and to provide time for students to discuss what they hear, and to write or draw in response to the reading. According to Smolkin and Donovan (2002), interactive read-alouds increase comprehension and promote active reading. We all use an interactive format when using read-alouds to frontload mathematical concepts and new vocabulary.

Patti uses the book *Spaghetti and Meatballs for All!* (Burns, 1997) to introduce a unit on measurement to her second graders. The book illustrates the problem encountered by a couple as they plan a reunion for their large, extended family. As each group arrives, they rearrange the original seating to accommodate all of the guests.

Once the story is enjoyed, Patti directs the students to work with her as they use the illustrations in the book to determine the area and perimeter for the different table arrangements. She wants the students to visualize the table arrangements and to represent them on a square centimeter grid. The example in Figure 4.1 shows how her class visualized the table arrangements. This is an excellent example of how teachers can use a familiar story format to introduce a new abstract concept. Teachers can find additional activities for using this book in an article by Moyer (2001).

Patti also uses *Amanda Bean's Amazing Dream* (Neuschwander, 1998) to prepare students for a unit on multiplication. The story is about a little girl who counts everything one by one, but learns in a dream that multiplying is another and faster way of counting. Prior to reading the book, Patti asks students to work with a partner to think about things that come in groups. These are then listed on a

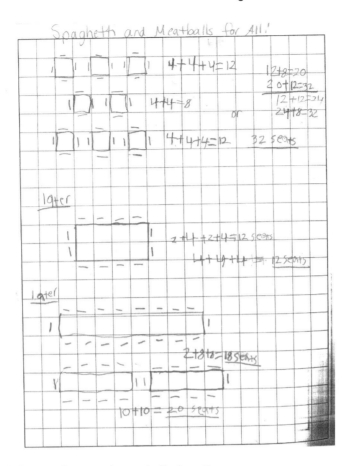

FIGURE 4.1. Spaghetti and meatballs for all!

chart prepared in advance of the lesson. This prereading activity prepares students to listen to the story carefully for things that come in groups. After first reading the story for enjoyment, Patti and the students go back through the text and find things that come in groups. She teaches the children that they do not have to reread an entire page of text; they can go straight to where they think they can find the information needed. This teaches them the strategy of skimming and scanning a text for specific information. In this instance, Patti is combining the teaching of math with the teaching of literacy.

Leitze (1997) recommends a variety of approaches for using literature as a springboard for the problem-solving portion of various mathematics lessons. In one of these the teacher seeks out books using the characters, objects, and settings to solve problems related to the concept. When introducing books, Young and Marroquin (2006) remind teachers to assess students' background knowledge and understanding of the topic to introduce specific vocabulary that may be new to students, and to connect the new learning to what students already know.

In the following example, the teacher uses questioning to help second graders negotiate their way through the book *Sand Castle Saturday* (Murphy, 1999). The questions help students articulate how their thinking changed as they gained more information.

TEACHER: What do we know?

TYLER: They are having a sand castle building contest.

CAROLINE: They have to measure.

TEACHER: Yes, they are measuring. Whose is the biggest? Be more specific. (*She added another question after they discussed whose is the biggest.*) What do we think now?

The questions helped the students keep track of new information. By the end of the discussion, students understood that we use standard units of measure to be accurate. They also learned that unusual objects such as shovels can be used to measure, but they have to be the same size to make good comparisons. Size matters. The idea of building sand castles is a wonderful example of using an everyday context to make concrete the importance of accuracy in measurement. However, without the discussion and questions, some children may have left the lesson as confused as the characters in the book were about equivalent measures.

Every teacher has his or her favorite read-alouds that they use every year because they are good reads enjoyed by the children and because they are powerful examples for extending students' understanding of mathematics. We have included a list of our favorite read-alouds in Appendix C.

Preparing Students for the Structure and Format of Math Textbooks

For most teachers the textbook determines the content, the sequence, and the activities for teaching mathematics. But it does not always provide the teacher with enough information to make the text accessible to all students. As just discussed, frontloading the content with literature read-alouds helps. Teachers can also demystify the text by explaining its internal organization, by demonstrating how to use the external text features, and by modeling active reading strategies for unpacking the content under study.

Demystifying the Text's Internal Organization

The structure of narrative text is familiar: there is a beginning, middle, and end. As the text becomes more sophisticated, authors include literary elements such as flashbacks and foreshadowing.

Teachers may not be as familiar with the structures commonly used in expository textbooks, especially because authors often use them in combination. The most common expository text structures include:

➢ Description

➢ Comparison/contrast

➢ Chronological order

➢ Problem and solution

➢ Procedural or process description (includes directions and explanation of steps in a process)

➢ Cause and effect

The overall structure of many elementary math texts includes a narrative section designed to provide a context for the content, and an expository section that includes key vocabulary, definitions, explanations, and procedures for using the particular mathematical operation or strategy (Hoyt, Mooney, & Parkes, 2003). The text may also include a section for sample problems, practice items, and additional narrative for checking understanding. Further, the text may include explanations where the authors combine descriptive, cause-and-effect, and comparison structures. Giving students a heads-up on how the author of the mathematics text organizes information can go a long way toward helping them understand it. Since many mathematics texts include a variety of structures within the same lesson, helping students label and understand the different structures and how they are integrated also helps them understand the information (Ogle, 1992).

The following is a typical math question.

> Imagine that your dad goes to the store to buy a tarp to cover the kitchen floor so he can paint the kitchen. Since he is a messy painter, he needs to make sure the whole floor is covered. How could he figure out how many square feet of tarp to buy?

The first part provides a narrative context for the math lesson under study. The main idea of the math problem comes at the end in the form of a question. Carole asked her third-grade students to read the math text to review the concept of area.

> Some surfaces are too large to cover with squares. It would take too long to count a large number of squares. To find the area of a rectangle . . . (Bell et al., 2001, p. 138)

The text explains the steps in the process for finding area. Next the text presents students with another problem in which they must calculate the area.

Blachowicz and Ogle (2001) suggest that teachers help students use the internal structure of a text to predict what they think the lesson will be about and to generate questions they think will be answered by the text. In the example above, students can predict that the author is going to provide information in the next section regarding how to figure out how much tarp will be needed.

Teachers can think aloud as they name the various structures used in the lesson and unit. Eventually, students can note the various structures using sticky notes. Duke and Bennett-Armistead (2003, p. 64) suggest the following sentence stems for helping students notice text organization: "I think this is organized by . . . " and, "This section talked about . . . so I think this next section will talk about . . . " For primary-grade students, it is enough to help them notice the different sections of the lesson. They can then predict what they think the new learning will be about before actually reading the text.

Teaching How to Read Charts, Graphs, and Other Features

Some standards-based textbooks include supplemental materials such as data banks, maps, posters, essays, and directions for playing math games. These print resources may contain features that present challenges for students without providing explicit instruction. In some cases, students read charts and tables from bottom to top or may determine their own starting point for text with sidebars, pictures, and captions. For example, Carole was working with one of her third-grade students to read a number grid. In the hundreds chart shown in Figure 4.2 the numbers go from one to one hundred in rows of ten. Reading down the grid, the numbers go up in value. However, when explaining the grid, teachers often say, "we are counting up," meaning that we are counting higher. Without clarification student confusion can result.

In order to follow directions for solving problems, explaining computation strategies, and for playing math games, students have to understand explanations and sequencing. They need to learn how to integrate the information found in

0	1	2	3	4	5	6	7	8	9
10	11	12	13	14	15	16	17	18	19
20	21	22	23	24	25	26	27	28	29
30	31	32	33	34	35	36	37	38	39
40	41	42	43	44	45	46	47	48	49
50	51	52	53	54	55	56	57	58	59
60	61	62	63	64	65	66	67	68	69
70	71	72	73	74	75	76	77	78	79
80	81	82	83	84	85	86	87	88	89
90	91	92	93	94	95	96	97	98	99
100									

FIGURE 4.2. Children learn to explain their computation methods using the hundreds chart.

tables and graphs with the information in the written text, which may include mathematical symbols and signs.

Students begin creating graphs and charts as early as kindergarten. They graph things such as how many students get hot or cold lunch, how many letters each child has in his or her name, and how many students like a particular kind of treat. The more students create their own graphs and charts, the easier it is for them to read these features when they meet more sophisticated models in their content textbooks. However, with each new form, teachers must again teach how to read the graph or chart so that students understand the information and can learn how to create similar graphs and charts on their own.

Moline (1995, p. 112) provides wonderful examples of graphs, charts, diagrams, and tables and describes how to help students read and construct their own versions of these text features. Moline states, "A table not only summarizes information; it also organizes it for us. This can be an advantage when we are searching for very specific information and it aids the scanning process." He suggests that teachers ask students to write out the information presented in the table or graph. This tells teachers what the students understand about the information presented. It also helps students to notice what information is provided in the graph or chart and how it differs from the same information provided in paragraph form.

Serafini (2004) suggests that teachers provide guided practice in recognizing and using visual features. After presenting examples of various features such as graphs, charts, diagrams, maps, headings, and labels students can be placed in small groups with each group assigned a particular feature. The group addresses each of the questions shown in Figure 4.3 and prepares a presentation about their feature for the class.

Because authors often present different information in graphic features than in the body of the text, activities like this help children understand the purpose of the

---

Ask students in small groups to analyze a particular feature (e.g., graph, chart, sidebar, picture and caption) and to share what they learn with the rest of the class. Use the following questions to guide students as they analyze the particular text feature.

1. What is the subject of the text feature?
2. Why do you think the author put it in there?
3. What can you learn about the subject in this feature?
4. How is the information presented?
5. What is challenging about reading this feature?
6. What strategies would you suggest for other readers?

FIGURE 4.3. Helping students understand format features of math texts. Data from Serafini (2004, p. 106).

graphic feature and highlight the need for them to use strategies for comprehending the information presented. They then have the task of figuring out how to integrate the information found in the graphic with the information presented in the body of the text. Mathematics texts often include graphic features as explanations for the material presented in the body. Students need to fully understand this concept.

As we will discuss in the next chapter, concept books can be used during reading to introduce students to graphic features and other visual elements. For example, Carole tried the above procedure with a group of third graders using the students' math book and some of the new math and literacy concept books. One student summarized the group's analysis of pictures and captions as follows:

> "You can see what the author means about comparing the height of a basketball player to [the height of stacked] basketballs and to [the height of] a girl. The picture showed the number of basketballs it took to reach the same height as the basketball player and the girl. The caption helps us see how tall the player is. The author probably included it because it would be hard to explain just using words. Our group used retelling to help explain how the author compared things to help us understand measuring height."

In the next chapter we discuss strategies for teaching students how to actively read math texts. These include the main math book and math problems as well as related math concept books.

CHAPTER 5

ACTIVELY READING MATH TEXTS

Students must be active and strategic when reading the math text because of its density and the necessity to pay attention to all of the words and symbols (Daniels & Zemelman, 2004). They need to use the same cognitive strategies that they use when reading in other content areas (National Reading Panel, 2002; Harvey & Goudvis, 2000; Marzano, Pickering, & Pollock, 2001) This includes using what they know about how to organize and remember new information. Students do not make this leap on their own.

In their study of exemplary primary teachers, Pressley, Allington, Wharton-McDonald, Block, and Morrow (2001) found that these teachers provided a great deal of coaching in addition to direct teaching and often used small groups to reinforce the learning. Coaching students to connect prior knowledge with new learning and to organize and remember information takes many forms.

Through our work with students we believe that the strategies shown in Figure 5.1 are most effective for students as they read the math text and solve math problems. We use coaching, direct teaching, and scaffolds to support students' flexible use of the strategies.

In Chapter 4, we described how teachers can use interactive read-alouds of appropriate math-related literature to guide students' use of many of the above strategies. But these strategies also need to be explicitly taught during math lessons. Further, a growing body of research (Pressley, 2006; Duke & Bennett-Armistead, 2003; Blachowicz & Ogle, 2001) suggests that students need to be taught to use these strategies in combination because it leads to greater gains. Students need to know what the strategies are (content knowledge) and why they are useful, know how to use them (procedural knowledge), and know when particular strategies might be most beneficial for meeting their needs (conditional knowledge).

- Thinking aloud while reading
- Connecting
- Paraphrasing
- Visualizing and drawing
- Inferring/predicting
- Summarizing and explaining
- Self-regulating, being metacognitive (checking that it makes sense)

FIGURE 5.1. Student strategies for actively reading math texts.

In this chapter, we provide examples of lessons, strategies, and instructional routines that teachers can use to help students remain active and engaged during the reading of the text. These are listed in Figure 5.2. These activities can be used to support students' reading and understanding of the math text in a whole-group setting or when working with students in small groups or pairs. The first part of this chapter focuses on active reading of the math text and math problems. The second part discusses how best to use informational math concept books.

- Scaffolds for Word Problems
    Reading Strategies Bookmark
    Genre–Reading Strategies Anchor Chart
    Word Problem Think Sheets
- Student Think-Alouds
- Using Questions
    Questioning the Author (QtA)
- Turn and Talk about Math Text
- Student Retelling
- Visualizing/Drawing
    Word Problem Think Sheets
    KWL
- Note Taking as a Reading Strategy
- Facts, Questions, and Response (FQR)
- Summarizing

FIGURE 5.2. Instructional routines for reading the math text.

READING MATH PROBLEMS

Scaffolds for Word Problems

We often find that students struggle to tell us what a math problem is about after reading it through. Therefore, to support students, we give them routines for taking the problem apart and for thinking about how the text is organized. We model the following steps for students many times: read; think; paraphrase; visualize; represent; solve; explain; and justify. We also teach them to ask questions at various points in the process. For example, we model how we question after paraphrasing: "Am I right? Did I say what the problem is about?" We model how to reread the problem after solving it to make sure that we answered the question that was asked: "Did I solve the problem?" In the process of modeling the strategies and inserting the questions in the process, we hoped to address Pressley's (2006) concern that students were not being taught how to self-regulate and use comprehension strategies as they read.

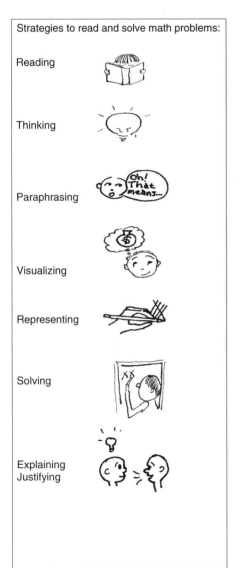

Math Reading Strategies Bookmark

We created the bookmark shown in Figure 5.3 to remind students of the process for understanding word problems. Initially, we tape the bookmark on their desks and eventually move it to their math folders. The bookmark was designed as a visual reminder of the process and as a scaffold for students to self-regulate comprehension of the problem.

In the following example, Peter, a third-grade student in Carole's class was working on the following subtraction story problem:

My mom gave me $5.00. I spent $0.68 on bananas and $1.59 on milk. How much did I spend? How much change did I get?

Peter said, "This doesn't make sense." This was a significant thing for a child to say. More often this kind of response comes in the form of, "I don't get it." Peter's response told Carole

FIGURE 5.3. Bookmark with math reading strategies.

that the work they had been doing with reading—connecting word problems to reading strategies—had made Peter aware of his own comprehension while reading word problems. He was beginning to self-regulate.

Carole praised Peter for noticing that the problem did not make sense to him. She moved close to him and reminded him of the strategies the class had practiced.

"Remember a strategy for understanding. Paraphrase the question. Paraphrase and draw or diagram each piece of information." Peter is a capable math student. So Carole decided that if he was asking for help, it probably indicated that everyone needed more support. She planned another lesson to model the paraphrasing and diagramming strategies again, and had children use the Word Problem Think Sheet in Figure 5.4.

Then in reading class Carole made the anchor chart in Figure 5.5 to show strategies the class has been practicing for various genres.

As Carole added the "Math Problem" entry to the chart and reminded the class

Name _____

Problem (number story) here:

What do we want to find out? (Paraphrase):

Information/details of the story:

	Diagram or picture:
One thing I know:	
Another thing I know:	
Another thing I know:	

FIGURE 5.4. Word Problem Think Sheet. Children use a Think Sheet as they read and understand the problem.

Genre	Strategy
Fantasy	Identify elements of fantasy and reality
Information	Identify main idea and details
Math Problem	Paraphrase Visualize

FIGURE 5.5. Genre–Strategy Anchor Chart.

that they were talking about reading, Hannah said, "You're kidding, right?" The class paused, thought, chuckled, and incorporated the joining of the math and literacy into their thinking.

Teaching Students to Think Aloud

We have already discussed thinking aloud as practiced by the teacher in the context of encouraging math talk and for interactive read-alouds. Students can also be taught to think aloud and in the process we teach them strategies for what to do when meaning breaks down. Thinking aloud (Davey, 1983) makes the invisible visible. Thinking aloud means that the reader articulates what he or she is thinking and doing while reading the text. Think-alouds can be used before, during, and after reading the text. The process is for the reader to stop reading at strategic points in the text and explain how he or she is processing and making sense of the text by:

➢ Making connections;

➢ Asking questions;

➢ Paraphrasing;

➢ Using fix-up strategies when something doesn't sound right or make sense (e.g., reread, read ahead, divide the word into syllables, use context clues);

➢ Inferring and predicting;

➢ Drawing or making a note to help remember what is occurring.

The teacher usually models the process first and then asks students try it out in pairs or in a guided reading of the text. According to Duke and Bennett-Armistead (2003, p. 59), thinking aloud is a powerful strategy and students' comprehension increases when they use it.

Blachowicz and Ogle (2001, p. 85) developed a rubric for analyzing students' think-alouds. Using the rubric can help teachers find out how students are processing text or discover where meaning breaks down, and figure out where they need to go next in planning mini-lessons for reteaching. We have altered the rubric slightly for use with math texts.

Analyzing Student Think-Alouds

Before reading: *Did the reader . . .*

➢ Notice cues for prediction, such as title, picture, heading, charts, graphs?

➢ Make some suitable prediction about the topic or concept?

➢ Bring up something already known about the topic or concept?

➢ Connect to like problems?

During reading: *Did the reader . . .*

➢ Comment on what was read?

➢ Ask questions to be clarified?

➢ Try to answer his or her own questions and clarify what didn't make sense?

➢ Relate what was being read to prior knowledge?

➢ Summarize and/or retell the gist up to that point?

➢ Check guesses or predictions?

➢ Reread or read ahead when trying to make sense?

➢ Use context for word meaning?

➢ Create and describe representations or visualizations?

➢ Begin to formulate a plan for solving the problem?

After reading: *Did the reader . . .*

➢ Summarize or retell?

➢ Respond?

➢ Critically reflect?

➢ Adjust the plan for solving the problem?

➢ Explain a possible solution to the problem?

➢ Justify thinking?

Teaching Students to Ask and Answer Questions

Some teacher educators (Harvey & Goudvis, 2000) suggest that questioning is at the heart of learning. Teachers use questions to activate interest and background knowledge, to assess student understanding, to pose interesting real-world problems, and to help students reflect on their learning. Heuer (2005, p. 52) suggests, "In addition to providing feedback about student understanding, questions also serve a mediating function, helping students discover what they know (or don't know) as they attempt to construct mathematical meaning." In their study of what constitutes high-quality instruction in math and science classes, Weiss and Pasley (2004, p. 26) list effective questioning as one of the indicators of such instruction. "Teachers' questions are crucial in helping students make connections and learn important mathematics and science concepts. Effective questioning—the kind that monitors students' understanding of new ideas and encourages students to think more deeply—was relatively rare in the mathematics and science classes we observed."

Because we need to help students develop their own questions, teachers model questioning during think-alouds about a topic before reading. They record their questions on an overhead, and then during reading they seek to clarify meaning and find answers to their questions. After reading, teachers model how they reread if they still have questions about the content or how they search for answers using other references, including other people.

Teachers can model questioning starting with " . . . I wonder . . . " or, "What if . . . " or, "What do you think? Will that work?" Many teachers and researchers have shared how they use and model questioning for students (Hoyt, 1999; McLaughlin & Allen, 2002; Oczkus, 2004; Johnston, 2004). Using question stems such as the above allows teachers to model higher-order questioning, which differs from the more common questions that emphasize understanding procedures or getting the right answer. However, it is important for teachers to let students know that they are modeling how and when they use questions as a way to help them understand what they are reading.

Marzano et al. (2001, pp. 113–114) suggest the following to guide teachers as they develop and model questions:

1. Cues and questions should focus on what is important as opposed to what is unusual.

2. "Higher-level" questions (see examples above) produce deeper learning than "lower-level" questions.

3. Waiting briefly before accepting responses from students has the effect of increasing the depth of students' answers.

4. Questions are effective learning tools even when asked before a learning experience.

As stated earlier, asking questions is also an important strategy students use to monitor their understanding and for generating discussion. Johnston (2004, p. 55) advises, "The ability or tendency to ask effective questions contributes a great deal to children's agency, and to their development of critical literacy."

"I love it when you question yourself. Were you right? Just because somebody asked you something, doesn't mean you were wrong. Just because an adult asked you a question, doesn't mean you were wrong when you spoke, OK? That's important. That's really important."

Questioning the Author (QtA)

Sandy used the Questioning the Author (QtA) strategy (Beck, McKeown, Hamilton, & Kucan, 1997) to help her fifth graders develop an active, strategic stance toward the text. She introduced "rates" by using a passage from the students' math book (Bell et al., 2002b, p. 96):

> The easiest fractions to understand are fractions that name parts of wholes and fractions used in measurement. In working with such fractions, it's important to know what the ONE or whole, is. For example, if a mile is the ONE, then ¾ mile describes 3 parts of a mile that has been divided into 4 equal parts.
>
> Not all fractions name parts of wholes. Some fractions compare two different amounts, where one amount is not part of the other. For example, a store might sell apples at 3 apples for 75 cents, or a car's gas mileage might be 160 miles/8 gallons.

In QtA, students learn to construct meaning while they read and that authors don't always present information in ways that are easily understood by readers. Key questions in the strategy involve asking the students, "What does the author mean?" "Why is the author telling us this?" "This is what the author is saying, but what does it mean?" and finally, "Can anyone say it differently so we can understand it better?" Figure 5.6 summarizes these key questions. The authors of the QtA strategy suggest using follow-up questions that begin with the student's response. Discussions generated with this type of question are called "query-driven" discussions because teachers use questions to *support* students' understanding of the text as opposed to *assessing* their understanding (Beck et al., 1997; Duke & Bennett-Armistead, 2003).

TEACHER: What does the author assume we know?

BEN: We know fractions. We remember that a fraction is less than one, like in ¼.

CLAIRE: You know, if you cut an apple into 4 parts, you have one.

- What does the author mean?

- Why is the author telling us this?

- This is what the author is saying, but what does it mean?

- Can anyone say it differently so we can understand it better?

FIGURE 5.6. Questioning the Author (QtA) strategy.

DESTINY: But the parts have to be equal.

TEACHER: Do the parts have to be equal to make the one whole?

CHARLES: I think we have to know what a whole is . . . there are different kinds of wholes, like a whole apple or a whole book.

MARGARET: The author assumes we know that the denominator tells you how many parts are in your whole.

DANIEL: And, measurement, we have to know measurement. You have to know cents.

DESTINY: But I don't get the ONE part of what the author means. It is mixing me up.

TEACHER: Can someone say it differently to help us understand what the author means?

CHARLES: The ONE is the whole and the ONE can be different. Not the number one, the whole thing so you have one like a whole apple would be ONE.

TEACHER: Is the author telling us something new?

TIFFANY: Yes, he says there are different kinds of fractions. I mean, like fractions can mean different things.

DESHAWN: Rates are fractions that compare. They compare different things like apples and money or miles and gallons.

TEACHER: So the author is describing rate and how it connects to fractions. The author also uses examples to provide details to make the description clearer. It helps us to understand this passage better if we know how the author is organizing the new information. Does anyone have a better way to present this information?

When Sandy asked students to think about what the author assumed they already understood, she helped them activate background knowledge for fractions. She knew that the students would probably be confused by the explanation of "one" in relation to fractions and rates and decided to focus the strategy work on getting at the important information. She used the students' responses as a springboard for asking additional QtA questions. She then articulated what they learned by restating the purpose of the questions and finally asking them to think about other ways of stating the same information. The students didn't have much to offer for restating in part because of the complexity of the information. However, just asking them to consider how they might present the same information lets them know that they can take a reflective stance on how the information is provided and that if they don't understand something, it is not necessarily their fault. Their lack of understanding may be a result of how the information is presented.

Turn and Talk about Math Text

In Chapter 2 we explained the "Turn-and-Talk Clock" as a way to get math talk started. When math talk is established, it can become a strategy for active reading of math text. In all our classrooms, we create student partnerships so when children are asked to turn and talk, they quickly know to whom they are supposed to turn.

After students individually read through a problem the first time, or after listening to the teacher or another student read the problem, they are asked to turn and talk to each other about what they are hearing or thinking. Students learn how different people think about a problem and how to solve it, or what the information means, or what questions they have about the information. This practice allows all voices in the classroom to be heard, not just the few children raising their hands when the teacher poses a question. It also allows students to rehearse math talk without having to share in front of everyone when thinking is just forming.

Teachers can begin by modeling the process with a partner, demonstrating how they paraphrase and think about what they heard. In the process of thinking, it is helpful to explain how the new information connects to what students already know. "This reminds me of . . . " is the language teachers can use to get started. Again, the important thing is to make students aware of the power of talking about their thinking and how the talk helps them self-regulate for meaning.

Student Retelling (Paraphrasing)

In the retelling strategy, students are asked to recall what they read or heard and to restate it in their own words, orally or in writing. When students use retelling as a comprehension strategy, they gradually learn to paraphrase and to understand that it is useful to be able to restate in their own words what they read. Through retellings, the teacher can assess how students use oral language, reconstruct a passage, prioritize, sequence, and remember information (Blachowicz & Ogle, 2001). Retellings also give an indication of students' ability to use text features and structures to organize, use, and remember information.

> CHRIS: I think I know how to play this game. But let's read the directions anyway.
>
> DEVON: So . . . I think we understand it. Let's retell it just to make sure. So . . . you roll the die 5 times. You write the numbers on these spaces (*pointing to the spaces in order*) and add it up.

Chris repeats Devon's retelling. In the process, he points out that the directions say to put the numbers in "any one of the spaces," and not, as Devon had thought, to put them in the spaces in the order that you roll them.

The interesting point of this exchange between the two students is that the less able reader, Devon, suggests the retelling. But, when the more experienced reader, Chris, repeats the retelling, he notices that the directions do not require the numbers to be placed in the order they are rolled. The teacher was thrilled to overhear this exchange between the two boys as the class had been working on retelling during Readering Workshop. This is an example of *transfer*—the ability to generalize learning from one situation to another. It also speaks to the power of retelling.

Brown and Cambourne (1990) demonstrate the power of retellings and provide examples of retellings using fiction and nonfiction short articles and charts. Students retell a piece of text in writing, then share with their partner, and together they construct a retelling based on what both students remember. Teachers who use retellings will notice that students begin to take on the language of the author and text as they become familiar with the process. Brown and Cambourne (1990, p. 10) refer to this as "linguistic spillover." When retelling is used in pairs or small groups during math time, we can expect that students will take on the mathematical language necessary for reading and understanding math texts. Eventually, the students will understand the relationship between a retelling and paraphrasing. They learn that when they retell information in their own words, they often use different words or phrases than the author used, but they don't change the meaning. They are paraphrasing what the author said. At the point that this connection is made explicit, the teacher may simply ask students to paraphrase the problem.

Visualizing, Drawing, and Representing

Visualizing, drawing, or other forms of representing are important strategies to use when reading math texts. Teachers and students read with a pencil in hand ready to draw the ideas presented, to create a plan for solving a problem, or to rework difficult text. The NCTM *Principles and Standards* (2000) require students to create and use representations to organize, record, and communicate mathematical ideas. As Heuer (2005, p. 52) acknowledges, "Mathematics is not only composed of words and symbols. It is also a pictorial language that uses visual models to communicate." Representations can also provide a window into students' understanding of the problem. Sharing visualizations and drawings can support students who are having difficulty by showing them how others approach a problem.

As we have found children needing help in explaining a problem and sorting out details, we have designed scaffolds for word problems such as the Think Sheet presented earlier in Figure 5.4 and the one in Figure 5.7, which isolates just the information and drawing elements for students. Supports such as these can help children read and understand the problem. If they are unable to create a representation, it may signal a lack of understanding. Students in our classrooms learn that they can ask someone for help: They may need to talk to their partners to help them create a visual image of the problem.

One of our fifth-grade teachers asked her students to visualize and draw the following problem as they worked their way to providing an explanation and proof of the solution.

Information in the Problem	
One thing I know:	Drawing:
Another thing I know:	Drawing:

FIGURE 5.7. Information in the problem. This scaffold helps students focus on identifying only the information in the problem and drawing representations for it.

A mole can dig a tunnel 300 feet long in one night. How many yards can a mole dig in three weeks? (Remember: 3 ft. = 1 yd.) (source unknown)

Students' drawings provide a quick assessment of who understands the problem and who needs additional support. The first student example shown in Figure 5.8 demonstrates clear understanding. The second one, Figure 5.9, a cute picture, indicates that the student did not read carefully, confused days and weeks, and does not understand what 3 ft. = 1 yd. means. As this example shows, visualizing and drawing does not necessarily help all students understand a problem. This is why it is important for students to know a number of strategies and use them in combination to comprehend a task. For example, it may have helped if students were asked to paraphrase the problem before visualizing and drawing.

Note Taking as a Reading Strategy

As we've described earlier, teachers often place anchor charts in front of the class to remind students of routines established for how to approach a math problem. In an online newsletter, a teacher named Laura Kump (*readinglady.com*) shared an instructional routine created with her second-grade students. It makes use of a note-taking strategy for helping students take apart and understand math word problems in order to solve them. The steps of the strategy are[1]:

Step 1   Read the entire problem.

Step 2   Try to access your prior knowledge. What is the problem about? Write that word below the problem and put a box around it.

---

[1]Adapted with permission from Laura Kump (*readinglady.org*).

What the problem looks like:

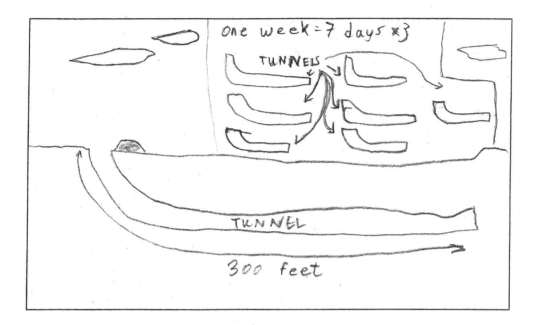

What the solution looks like:

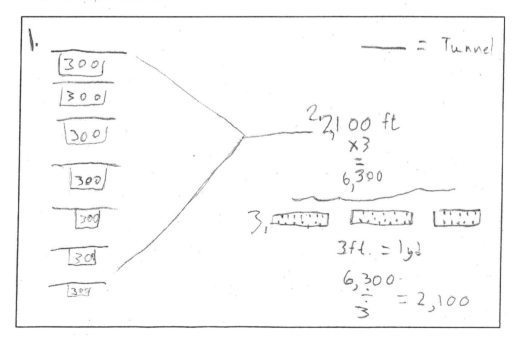

FIGURE 5.8. Drawing of the "mole" problem clearly understood.

What the problem looks like:

What the solution looks like:

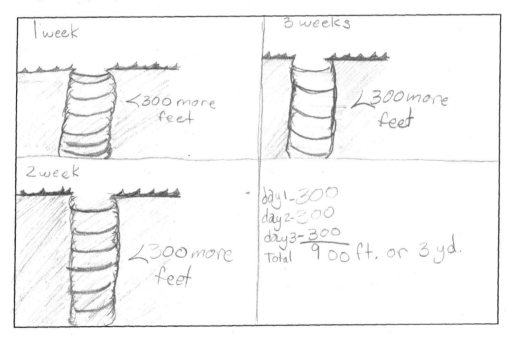

FIGURE 5.9. Drawing of the "mole" problem not understood.

Step 3   Reread the problem, sentence by sentence and put a box around the important clues. List the important clues below the problem. (This allows students to remove them from the body of the text where they can hopefully see the problem more clearly.)

Step 4   Think. Do you understand the question? Restate part of it below the problem.

Step 5   Come up with a plan to solve your problem. What will you need to do with the important clues you have collected?

Step 6   Solve the problem.

Step 7   Explain in writing how you worked through the problem.

Carole used a version of these steps with her third graders on the following problem.

> Corinne and Ella put their money together to buy tickets to the circus. The total cost of the tickets is $28. Ella pays $6 less than Corinne. How much does each girl pay?

This is the class's first time using the note-taking strategy and Carole provides a significant amount of scaffolding. The children have written the problem at the top of an otherwise blank paper while Carole shows a copy of the problem on an overhead transparency. First the class identifies the question (main idea) and paraphrases it. Carole writes: "What we want to find out."

TEACHER (*thinking aloud*): What is the main idea of this text? Hmmm . . . it is a question . . . the main idea is that we want to find out something. What is it?

STUDENT: How much money does each girl pay?

Carole underlines that sentence and asks students to underline the question on their papers.

How much money does each girl pay?

Then Carole points out the word *each* and asks the class what it means. Several children offer explanations. "It means every one." "Every one separately." This develops into a bit of a discussion. Two children come to the front of the class. Carole demonstrates by giving them each a pencil. They talk about the significance of the word *each*. Carole gets an index card, writes the word, and displays it in a prominent spot on the word wall.

STUDENT: We're trying to find out two things.

TEACHER: Yes! This question is really two questions. What are the two questions?

The class together decides that the two questions are:

"How much does Corinne pay?" and "How much does Ella pay?"

Carole has them write these questions under the problem, and enclose them in a box.

TEACHER (*thinking aloud*): Now that we have the main idea, what are the details? What is the information in the problem?

Carole is pointing out the connections between "main idea" (question) and "details" (information). They have discussed these connections explicitly in a previous lesson.

STUDENT: Ella pays $6 less than Corinne.

TEACHER: So . . . I wonder what that really means. . . . Ella pays $6 less than Corinne. I want to paraphrase that to say it in my own words. Can you help me?
    Student suggestions: "Ella pays less than Corinne." "Ella pays $6 less." "Corinne pays $6 more." "They both have money but there is a difference." "They do not have the same amount of money."

They finally decide to write:

"Corinne and Ella both pay money." "Corinne's money is $6 more than Ella's."

TEACHER: Now I need to make a diagram of that so I will really understand it. How about this?

Carole calls it a "diagram" rather than a "picture," mostly because they have just been learning about the text feature of diagrams in the context of reading science informational texts. Carole draws two rectangles that are the same, then adds on to the second rectangle and labels the added-on portion "$6" as depicted in Figure 5.10.

The children do not like Carole's representation. So she quickly proposes another: two stick figures. Each is holding a money bag. They look the same. She labels them "E" for Ella and "C" for Corinne. In Corinne's other hand she draws a second money bag and labels it "$6."

What we want to find out.

How much does Corinne pay?
How much does Ella pay?

- Corinne and Ella have money.
- Corinne's money is more than
  Ella's.

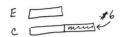

- Circus costs $28.00

- girls put their money
  together

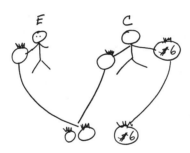

- All the money together is
  enough for the circus.
  $28.00

[O O] + 6 = 28

[22] + 6 = 28

[11 + 11] + 6 = 28

Corinne pays $17.00
Ella pays $11.00

FIGURE 5.10. Circus problem diagram.

STUDENTS: Ah! (*They like it!*)

So Carole asks them to draw something similar on their papers. They continue in this manner, listing all the information and drawing it. Carole then gets a student to come up and draw a circus tent labeled with the cost: "$28."

Girls put their money together.

Carole draws two girls with money bags again, this time with lines connecting the money bags as shown in Figure 5.10.

All the money together is enough for the circus: $28.

By now the fastest math thinkers in the class have figured out how much the two girls had paid. But they stay engaged in this process of how the class is thinking and representing. Although Carole thinks it would be very interesting to pursue finding out how those who have it figured out have done so, she knows they are getting pressed for time. (Carole thinks aloud.)

TEACHER: Here's one way to do it. How could we show this information with a number model?

Carole draws: $\boxed{\bigcirc + \bigcirc}$ + 6 = 28

TEACHER: So, the things inside the box plus 6 equal 28. So, the things inside the box equal 22.

At this point, Peter, who figured it out several steps prior to this, says: "But, we have to answer two things: How much does *each* girl pay?"

TEACHER: So . . . How much is in each of these circles?

STUDENTS: 11! Because that is half of 22!

Now everyone is leaping about because they all figure it out all at once.

ALL: We got it!

Corinne pays $17.
Ella pays $11.

After the lesson, Ahmed, Carole's most fragile math student, is flushed with excitement. "Mrs. Skalinder, that lesson made our minds think and it was fun!" Figure 5.11 summarizes Carole's version of the note-taking process.

1. Read the entire problem.
2. What do we want to find out? [*The main idea is a question.*]
3. Think. Do you understand the question? Restate part of it below the problem. [*This asks students to paraphrase.*]
4. What are the details [*i.e., information*]? Reread the problem, sentence by sentence and put a box around the important clues. List the important clues below the problem.
5. What will you need to do with the important clues you have collected? [*This ask students to visualize, diagram, or use manipulatives to represent the details of the problem.*]
6. How do we show this information with a number model?
7. Solve the problem.
8. Explain how you worked through the problem in writing.

FIGURE 5.11. Note-taking steps for solving a math problem.

We often find that good examples, like the one from the Reading Lady, are shared when they have been worked on over time and developed to a level beyond where most teachers start when using a new strategy. However, teachers sharing ideas like this one help us to increase our repertoire of teaching strategies and ultimately help our students become better mathematicians.

USING INFORMATIONAL MATH CONCEPT BOOKS

Publishers have been creating and publishing concept books to help students understand concepts in social studies and science for several years. They have made it possible for teachers to differentiate instruction and to expand on ideas glossed over in science and social studies courses. The addition of math titles is relatively new and welcomed. These books allow teachers to blur the lines between reading and content instruction across disciplines. Many of the science informational books have mathematical content as well. These very engaging texts have a foundation in math, yet need teacher explanation to make them most meaningful to students.

According to Duke and Bennett-Armistead (2003, p. 16), informational books differ from other types of nonfiction in purpose, features, and format. Their primary purpose is to convey information "with particular linguistic features such as headings and technical vocabulary to help accomplish that purpose." These texts often include visuals such as pictures, labels, captions, and may include graphics such as diagrams, charts, and tables. This sounds a lot like a math textbook. As with math texts, knowing and recognizing a book's organizational structure and use of navigational features such as the table of contents, headings, and bold print help students understand the topic better because they have a framework for remembering the new information.

Duke and Bennett-Armistead (2003) go on to say that informational text typically addresses a whole class of things. Informational math books that fit this criterion have titles such as, *Which is the Tallest?* (Pullen, 2004) and *Comparing Sizes and Weights* (Nguyen, 2006). Finally, these texts come in many different formats, including books, magazines, and online versions.

These texts can be used in a variety of ways: as read-alouds that are then placed in centers for additional exploration and activities; in shared reading to launch a new strategy for reading and understanding informational text; and if enough copies, in guided reading. Many students choose these books during independent reading because of their visual appeal and because they build on students' natural interest in the real world. However, because we often read informational texts in a nonlinear fashion, students need skills and strategies for effectively and efficiently accessing information available in these texts.

The strategies readers need to process informational text include:

➤ Activating background knowledge

➤ Setting a purpose for the reading

➤ Reading the table of contents

➤ Predicting and inferring

➤ Decoding new and specialized vocabulary

➤ Skimming and scanning for specific information

➤ Making connections

➤ Using the index and glossary

➤ Checking and monitoring for understanding

➤ Integrating the visual and graphical information with the narrative information

➤ Summarizing and synthesizing the information

In the following sections, we offer examples of how to make explicit connections for children between the ideas embedded in the informational text and the mathematical concepts we expect to develop in daily math lessons.

Facts, Questions, and Responses Strategy

Harvey and Goudvis (2007) make the point that when students are reading nonfiction they often get bogged down in details that are new information but not necessarily important to getting the gist. They suggest that the first step to active reading is acknowledging when we learn something new. Students need help processing this information along with putting these facts in perspective to the reading. The Facts, Questions, and Responses (FQR) strategy (Harvey, 1998) helps address these reader challenges. It provides a graphic structure in which students can record new facts, pose questions that the new facts may generate, and pay attention to their responses to the information. The latter is the often unvoiced recognition that something is new, or confusing, or contradictory to what was previously known. The written response mirrors what is going on in the head of the learner (metacognition). This is one graphic organizer that teachers may find especially helpful for making the point that students must listen to the inner conversation that is going on in their heads when they are reading actively as opposed to merely reading words. The form provides a scaffold to help students stay active. If they have no response or questions, they are probably just reading words.

Through this process, students can get to the important information while working through the interesting details. Students use an FQR sheet with three columns headed, Facts, Questions, and Responses, respectively. This serves as the springboard for conversation about what is the important information provided by the author. Students also begin to understand how headings, words in bold print, and other text features signal what is important. The FQR three-column form can be put on the chalkboard, or on an overhead transparency. The teacher models how to read a section of text and indicates in the column whenever he or she reads a new fact. The teacher may have a question about that fact or a response like, "I didn't know that," which is then recorded in the question or response column. The teacher continues reading and thinking aloud while recording new facts, questions, and responses. After modeling a few of the fact-gathering and questioning or responding entries, the teacher invites students into the process. Students are asked to read the next section and use their individual FQR sheets to record their thinking. The teacher circulates among the students as they work their way through the next section of text conferring with children individually and noting who might have a good question or response to share. This gradual release of responsibility provides the necessary scaffold for students to use the FQR on their own.

Carole used the concept book, *Crunching Numbers* (Jonhson, 2004), during the literacy block to launch the FQR strategy. This was part of a reading unit on determining importance and was linked to a discussion of estimating in a math unit on multidigit addition and subtraction. Carole has found that third graders often have difficulty understanding why one estimates in the real world. It takes

Facts	Questions	Responses
Estimating is a number-crunching strategy.	How can he estimate?	This sounds like an interesting job.
Monarchs can migrate thousands of miles.		

FIGURE 5.12. Fact, Question, and Response Sheet for reading *Crunching Numbers*.

talk and examples to help them see the purpose of estimating. She used the concept book to connect the children with a real-world example of how scientists use estimating to determine how the monarch butterfly population changes from year to year. She introduced the FQR strategy in a whole-group format using the chalkboard. Figure 5.12 shows what the recorded Facts, Questions, and Responses (FQR) sheet looked like.

Summarizing and Inferring

Students need support and lots of practice before they can summarize independently. Summarizing is one of the strategies students use to restate and paraphrase a problem before they begin to formulate a solution. As teachers, we have children use drawing, writing, and thinking sheets and talk to summarize the math ideas. Sometimes, we use think-aloud language such as, "I'm thinking the author is saying or asking . . . " as we help students read through text. Patti started having her second-grade students summarize through think-alouds. She first modeled how she was thinking through the reading of the book, *Sand Castle Saturday* (Murphy, 1999).

> *Now I think*: The shovels are different sizes so the children are using different measurement units. What do you think? Turn and talk.
> *Now I am thinking*: The lifeguard is showing how to use inches or standard measurement to measure things because the children didn't understand why their measurements weren't right.

The sentence stem "Now I think . . . " provides a necessary scaffold for students to summarize the information gained thus far. The additional language of "Now I am thinking . . . " shows how thinking changes with additional information. The stems also allow students to infer based on current information and to add to their thinking as they learn more.

When students infer during reading of narrative text, they are taught to use what they know plus information from the text to make sense of what the author is saying even when it is not directly stated. In math lessons, however, inference, according to O'Brien and Moss (2004, p. 293), can also mean "generating new knowledge out of old knowledge." For example, given a set of data points, students can estimate or infer beyond the data points once they have discovered a pattern. The students continually summarize based on additional information.

Using Concept Books to Teach Text Features

Carole also used *Crunching Numbers* (Johnson, 2004) to help students focus on the navigational features of informational texts such as table of contents, headings, bold words, and specialized vocabulary, graphs, maps, inserts, and glossaries. Because the book was so engaging, it was easy to talk about how to use and "read" the features and incorporate the graphic information into the narrative portion of the text. This again provided an opportunity to teach how mathematicians read and write in the real world.

Carole modeled reading and writing in response to using books from the series Math in Science or Math in Social Studies published by National Geographic: *Numbers and You* (O'Sullivan, 2004a), *Animal Records* (Russell, 2004), *The Speedy Cheetah* (Elliott, 2004), *Giraffes* (Huntingdale, 2004), and *Protecting Sea Turtles* (O'Sullivan, 2004b). Each one presented opportunities to model writing a subtraction problem using comparing. For example, in *Giraffes,* there is a picture of a giraffe, a narrative section on how much food giraffes eat, and an insert called "Do the Math." Students are asked to measure their arm and determine if it is shorter or longer than a giraffe's tongue.

Carole modeled noticing how the information in the photographs supports the information in the narrative portion of the text. Together, they talked about the insert and why the authors included it in the text. They then did the math.

Because the class did a bit of work in each of the books before they were placed in centers, the students were anxious to go to the centers with their partners and read more about each of the topics. The beautiful photographs and sample math activities kept the partners focused and engaged for long periods of time.

Using *A Walk in the Rainforest* (Novakowski, 2005) with her second graders Patti modeled how to find the big ideas in a text and to use text features such as a map to answer questions. She demonstrated how to find math ideas in informational text and how to formulate questions around those ideas. Students then worked with their partners to find the math ideas in their chosen text and to formulate their own questions. Students used a form titled "Book Conversations" to record their math ideas and questions, then exchanged books and answered the questions developed by the first set of partners.

Jonah read *Tim's Ice Cream Store* (Griffiths & Clyne, 2005). He wrote:

1. Tim uses a tally to keep track of what he sells.
2. He uses a tally to know what flavor of chocolate was the most popular.

He wrote the following questions:

1. What flavor didn't sell the most?
2. What flavor did Tim sell the least?

Jonah's partner, Jon, read *Games Kids Play* (Griffiths & Clyne, 2004). He followed the same format with facts and questions. One of Jon's questions was, "Is chess like math? Jonah answered, "A chess board is like a checkers board. So, on a checkers board you have arrays. Games are like math because some of them have arrays and some have numbers." Jonah was learning to use the language of mathematics.

The terms *tally, most, least,* and *arrays* are important for understanding and solving math problems. Patti fosters a sense of inquiry and interest by having students read different books and then provides an opportunity to use math vocabulary in authentic ways just by asking students to look for facts and to generate questions.

Shared Reading

Shared reading is a practice teachers use to explain a strategy, to show how to read and understand a text feature, to model a process, and to provide a common experience for all students before moving the same process into guided and independent reading. In shared reading, the teacher uses a big book or part of a text on an overhead transparency so that all students are able to see the text at the same time. While the strategy is often used in a whole-group setting, it can also be used with small groups.

Carole uses shared reading to demonstrate the text features found in the book, *The Speedy Cheetah* (Elliot, 2004). She displayed the table of contents, index, glossary, and one of the line graphs on an overhead transparency. She brought the students in close so that she could observe them and make quick adjustments as they participated in the shared experience. The author of the text used interesting chapter headings such as "Largest" and "Slowest," allowing Carole to talk about these terms in relation to math problem solving and to point out how authors like to make chapter titles interesting. She also pointed out that sometimes, in their effort to be interesting and clever, authors do not give readers enough information to know what the chapter may be about. Carole talked to the students about the need to infer and predict what they think the chapter might be about and then to go to the chapter to confirm or revise their predictions.

The teachers also use shared reading to introduce students to the KWL strategy (Ogle, 1986) described earlier in Chapter 3. This strategy is helpful for students to use as they read informational text. It provides a framework to record students' questions after helping them identify what they know about a topic. Some mathematics teachers change the "K" to a "P" (Predict what this unit/lesson will be about) and then add the other two columns. Once they have learned it in a shared-reading format, students can use the KWL or PWL format during partner and independent reading.

Guided Reading

Elementary teachers are familiar with the small-group differentiated instructional model called "guided reading." In guided reading, the teacher selects a text with a specific purpose in mind for a particular group of students. During the lesson, the teacher prompts and guides students to apply recently learned strategies on new text that is at just the right reading level. Intermediate teachers use flexible grouping to avoid tracking students into ability groups. They just need to be sure to use a text that is at a level easy enough for the lowest reader in the group. The purpose of the guided reading is to scaffold and guide student use of a particular strategy so that eventually they can then apply the strategies independently in books that are at an appropriately challenging level for each student.

The informational books we have used in guided reading lessons were specifically chosen to give students practice in using text features, in reading for fluency, and in reading about math applications in the real world. Guided reading provides teachers with a structure to support student use of these strategies and to teach about text features before they are encountered in more difficult text such as the math textbook.

For example, Patti used *Pigs on the Move* (Axelrod, 1991) in guided reading to help students apply what they knew about sequencing and determining time. The particular group was having trouble understanding time and time zones. Students used chart paper to write the time next to the event that happened in the story as they were reading it. Students also needed help to read and understand the names of cities and terms such as "city by the bay," and "mile-high city." This is a good book to use for additional practice in reading the clock and telling time. In the process of reading the text, students learned not only to read the numbers, but also to understand the relationship between time and sequence in a story.

Another group read "The Little Red Hen" in *Funny Fairy Tale Math* (Franco, 2001). This text is interesting because students are introduced to procedural text in the form of a recipe. Through reading the story, Patti exposed students to math concepts such as capacity, weight, and elapsed time. Students used retelling to remember the important events in the story. Eventually, they realized many of the questions posed in the text could be solved using the recipe card without rereading the text.

Guided Reading and Readers' Theatre

Teachers often use reader's theatre to help students work on fluency. It is an enjoyable way to get students to reread the same text multiple times. Knowing that this is performance reading helps the students to pay more attention to punctuation, phrasing, and expression—all important contributors to comprehension. Patti used a scripted reader's theatre book, *No Math Day at School* (Kramer, 2003), with a group of second-grade students in a small-group guided reading lesson. She used this text with this particular group of students to teach the format of reader's theatre: characters' names are followed by a colon and then the words the character said. Words such as *said, replied,* and *yelled,* which usually indicate some action by the character, were not included in the script. Patti also worked with the students to understand how the exclamation point is used to show feeling or to emphasize a point. She was able to teach to several of the language arts standards as well as address the NCTM Communication Standard (2000): analyze and evaluate the mathematical thinking and strategies of others.

Patti guided the students to make predictions of the content by looking at a list of words and phrases from the text: *no math day, bake sale, recess, money, counting,* and *subtraction.* The students then generated sentences using the words to tell what they thought the story would be about. This strategy is often referred to as "Story Impressions" (Blachowicz & Fisher, 2002, p. 52).

Julia wrote:

> Maybe Mrs. Hamton said there's *no math day* because they're taking a break from math. And they're having a *bake sale* at *recess* to earn *money* for some books in the library. They are having trouble *counting* money.

Patti helped the children understand that the characters' mathematical thinking was faulty: they need math class to know how to *subtract* money from a dollar. Finally, the group looks back at the list of ways the characters use math and decides counting money, telling time, and adding and subtracting are the big areas of math covered in the play.

Putting It All Together

Math texts present challenging reading to many of our students. Often it is not the decoding but rather the vocabulary, concepts, and text structure that provide the challenges. In this chapter, we offer a variety of strategies for addressing the challenges: frontloading the concepts and vocabulary, creating opportunities for active learning, helping students use routines and strategies to understand and remember information, including informational trade books to supplement the learning of new concepts, and offering hands-on lessons.

We recommend using a variety of grouping strategies to address the various needs of students as they grapple with new concepts, need additional instruction and practice, and seek to find math applications in the real world.

Grouping students in a variety of ways allows us to differentiate instruction. We use whole-group formats to build common mathematical knowledge, small-group and partner reading to reinforce concepts and problem-solving strategies, and individual work to uncover and assess student understandings.

These various grouping arrangements also allow us to gradually release responsibility for the learning. Teacher-supported shared and guided reading of the math text makes way for partner and small-group applications of the learning until we are primarily observing and reviewing student work in journals, listening to student explanations and justifications, and inviting students to orally share their questions and ideas with others.

We move now into vocabulary, an area deserving of its own chapter. We want to help students move from describing the mathematics they are learning through concrete experiences to using more formal mathematical language. Knowing and understanding the language of mathematics is key to effective mathematical communication and to comprehending math texts.

CHAPTER 6

LEARNING MATH VOCABULARY

"Please can't we stay in from recess to keep doing math?"
"Now math is my favorite subject! It used to by my *least* favorite subject. Wow!"
"Math is easier now. I didn't used to like it!"
"Let's have a math party!"

Comments like these begin to emerge late in September in Carole's third-grade class. They indicate that the experiences connecting literacy and math are having a considerable effect on children's confidence in math lessons. Work on vocabulary words can build student understanding for critical math concepts and the excitement generated for math words brings math literacy to the forefront of the class's thinking. This excitement transfers to the vocabulary of other content areas and all word study for the entire year.

According to the NCTM *Principles and Standards* (2000), students should use the language of mathematics to express mathematical ideas precisely. To do so, students must have a firm grasp of that language. This develops gradually. Murray (2004, p. 4) describes middle school students who still struggle with basic concepts and don't even have the language for expressing their confusion. She states, "It is my conviction that an important way to ensure the development of mathematically powerful students is to build a strong foundation in mathematics vocabulary."

Usiskin (1996, p. 232) laments the fact that we teach mathematics as if it is different from learning other languages. "Like most modern languages, mathematics is both oral and written and can be either informal or formal. Like all languages, communication is one of its major purposes. Like all languages, it not only describes concepts but helps shape them in the mind of the user. That is, mathematics is *like* a language because it *is* a language like any other." Adams (2003, p. 787) states that "When we pass up opportunities to focus children's attention on mathematics as a language and not just something we do, children may miss the underlying concepts of mathematics that would enhance and reinforce their understanding." We believe that school must provide the lessons, resources, and motivation for students to enter into the study of mathematical language as a vital, interesting area, worthy of their attention because it helps them solve real-world problems.

How then do we create this interest? What does the instruction look like when we do as Usiskin suggests: immerse students in the language and start early? There is compelling evidence in the research and from our own classroom experiences that teaching mathematics content vocabulary needs to be a priority. Over the years, we have focused on three areas that pose the greatest challenges for our students: vocabulary terms specific to the discipline, words with multiple meanings, and "little" words that cause confusion (e.g., *each, left, all*, etc.). In trying to improve our instruction for addressing these challenges, we turned to the research and learned that some instructional strategies and routines are more effective than others. The work of Blachowicz and Fisher (2002, p. 7) has greatly influenced our work and we use their guidelines to plan for effective vocabulary instruction:

> ➢ Immerse students in words for both incidental and intentional learning by building a word-rich environment.
> ➢ Help students develop as independent word learners.
> ➢ Use strategies that teach vocabulary, but that also model good word-learning behaviors.
> ➢ Use assessment that matches the goal of instruction.

In Chapter 1 we described strategies for building a math word-rich environment including word walls, number lines, anchor charts, and activities to connect math with the real world. Throughout this chapter, we will describe ways to implement the other guidelines above. Our overall aims are to engage students so that they enjoy mathematics, to teach important mathematics vocabulary, and to address some of the relevant challenges for using the math text.

FROM INCIDENTAL TO INTENTIONAL VOCABULARY LEARNING

What does it means to "know" a word? Many researchers (Blachowicz & Fisher, 2002; Daniels & Zemelman, 2004; Beck, McKeown, & Kucan, 2002; Marzano, 2004) suggest that there is a continuum of learning. Initially, one knows little of a word's meaning, perhaps just the label. With repeated exposure, one progresses to knowing what the word means in a particular context. Moving farther along the continuum, one learns how to use the word appropriately in speech and writing. Finally, the learner develops a deep understanding of the word that includes nuanced and assorted meanings. When we have an expanded definition of a word, we are able to come up with an appropriate understanding in context.

Ball and Bass (2001) suggest that students progress from creating an emergent definition of a word to developing a "working" definition. Then, as they encounter more sophisticated mathematical concepts, the working definition is not enough and must be expanded to understand the concept more deeply. Ball and Bass provide an excellent discussion of this using the concept of even and odd numbers, moving from a simple understanding of what even and odd numbers are to expanding the idea to include negative numbers and fractions. The working definition must then be expanded to understand the concept of even and odd as it relates to more sophisticated knowledge of numbers.

Defining "Definition"

Before going further, it is important to clarify what we mean by *definition*. Many researchers and teachers, including Beck et al. (2002), Blachowicz and Fisher (2002), Marzano (2004), and Murray (2004), speak to the problems associated with dictionary definitions. Beck et al. (2002, p. 34) describe a number of the problems associated with such definitions:

> "Weak differentiation—the target word is not sufficiently different from other similar words.
>
> The definition is stated in vague language that provides little information.
>
> The meaning often can be interpreted differently than the intended meaning.
>
> Definitions often contain too much information.
>
> They use familiar words in unfamiliar ways.
>
> They do not offer enough guidance in how all the information provided should be integrated.

Given these problems, we agree that it is probably more accurate to use the term *explanation* for describing how we teach word meanings prior to using the dictionary. We know that simply giving students a definition or having them look words up in a dictionary will not provide them with enough information to understand the term. If we expect students to be able to explain the term and give examples of it, we need to plan an instructional sequence that will lead them to an understanding of the concepts underlying the terms. We can then provide supportive instruction for how to use the dictionary or glossary: Students can compare their emerging definitions with that of the dictionary, noting similarities and differences, discuss what the differences may mean, and perhaps make revisions to their definitions.

We want to create situations in which students find that they need to use the correct math terminology to provide clear and precise explanations of their thinking and solutions to problems. Once we do that, we will also need to create many opportunities for students to hear, see, write, and use the words. Marzano (2004, p. 73) puts it this way, "To understand the word at deeper levels, however, students require repeated and varied exposures to words, during which they revise their initial understandings."

Many of the strategies we describe in this chapter not only teach math vocabulary but also function as assessments. This is especially true of vocabulary activities that ask students to both draw and write. These can give teachers a snapshot of the students who understand and those who are struggling with a term. One of Marzano's characteristics of effective direct vocabulary instruction is that students must represent their knowledge of words in linguistic and nonlinguistic ways. He provides compelling research on the effectiveness of having students represent words in both ways: language-based and imagery-based.

For example, after providing some initial background building and introducing concepts for a new math unit, Sandy asks her fifth-grade students to write each new word on an index card and then create a drawing of the word on the back. The drawing provides a memory cue for the students. Students also look through their texts and note where they can find additional information for the terms on their cards. They approach the task with a keen eye toward finding out more about the words. On the next day, students are asked to form groups to share and explain their drawings. As they work through a unit, students revise their pictures and develop an emerging definition of the word. About midway through the unit students write a sentence for the target word on the same side of the card as the picture. This practice allows for repeated exposure and an opportunity to interact with the words again. Then, in partners, students play word games with the cards and quiz each other using a cloze technique, again interacting with the words. Students read their sentence to one another leaving out the target word. The partner must select the correct term to complete the sentence.

Selecting Words to Study

Blachowicz et al. (2006) recommend teaching the words that are directly related to the unit of study in content learning. This is good advice. Some words are important to the math unit and difficult for students to learn indirectly. As we mentioned earlier, publishers usually label mathematical ideas from the start, before students have an opportunity to work with the underlying concepts. Therefore, one of the first things teachers can do is select math words for vocabulary study being mindful of which words need exploration and which words can be introduced prior to the unit. We recommended this in our discussion of planning for math–literacy integration in Chapter 1. Adding a few key math words to vocabulary instruction in advance of a math unit is highly effective.

A second, difficult task is to decide how to teach the words so that students are actively engaged in learning the words and in understanding the relationships among the words in a unit of study. Blachowicz and Fisher (2002) document a number of studies where students chose words for independent word learning. In each of these studies, they found that students chose challenging words and successfully learned them. Regarding ELL students, they cite the work of Jiminez (1997) who explains that self-selection is critical to understanding what words are confusing to the students. However, with respect to content learning, Blachowicz and Fisher (2002) suggest collaborative word choice whereby the teacher, as well as the students, contributes words for study, especially when the content includes difficult and new concepts. In each of the following activities, the teacher initially selects the words for study, and then collaborates with students in determining which words need more attention and will be studied further.

Marzano (2004) states that the number of terms that can be addressed in a program of direct vocabulary instruction is limited. Thus, the teacher's task is not only to select the words, but to be aware that students are also learning words in other content areas and, therefore, that the number of words to be learned must be reasonable.

Publishers often provide a list of the important terms for each unit of study. We select words for deeper study by using the vocabulary list from the publisher, along with the list of mathematical words provided by the state and observations of students' use of language. We then teach strategies for learning the words in much the same way that we teach comprehension strategies: explicit instruction, guided practice, and independent use.

STRATEGIES FOR DIRECT VOCABULARY INSTRUCTION

As with any teaching–learning cycle, it is important for teachers to decide on the sequence of activities that will be used to move students along the continuum of learning. Again we refer to Blachowicz et al. (2006, p. 528) to help us think about what to do with the terms to be taught directly. "Learners are actively involved in the generation of word meanings, rather than as passive receptors of information. This includes the integration of their prior knowledge with new information as well as building semantically related categories of words and concepts." Additionally, we know that we must provide definitional explanations as well as contextual information about the words as we expose students to new terminology.

Math-o-Lanterns

Patti begins by first assessing her second graders' knowledge of the following words from first grade: *circle, triangle, square, rectangle, hexagon, trapezoid, rhombus, and pentagon.* Each student has a paper with eight boxes on it. The teacher says a word and the students draw the picture of the shape in one the boxes. Patti plans to do this activity during word study time and to add these words to the word wall after the class discusses them. As a follow-up, she plans an art activity called "math-o-lanterns." This art project consists of paper pumpkins, glue, and geometric shapes made from colored paper. The faces are made with paper geometric shapes. The students write the name of the shapes on the geometric pieces of paper. This activity reinforces geometric vocabulary specifically for two-dimensional shapes. Patti plans to do this activity at the art center.

Geometry Name Tags

For the second-grade geometry unit (in the math block), Patti makes name tags for new vocabulary words. Each name tag has the geometric term on one side and the meaning on the other. Patti makes sure that the class studies the same number of words as the number of students in the class so each student can be given a name tag with a different word on it. Then, instead of calling students by their names, she calls them by their geometry word. For instance, "Tyler, please pass out the paper" changes to, "Prism, please pass out the paper."

Concept Sorts

For her fifth-grade students Sandy uses a concept sort activity to begin the year's work with word study. She looks at the beginning units of study in math, science, and social studies and then selects a short list of words that she knows the students will soon encounter in their reading in each content area.

The school in which Sandy teaches has a word study program that uses sorting as a way to get students actively involved in word study and paying attention to word patterns and meanings. In a concept sort, students are given a collection of words and are asked to sort them into groups. Teachers can provide an open sort or a closed sort. In an open sort, students sort the words and then determine a category for each group of words. In a closed sort, the teacher gives students the categories for sorting. Giving students the categories provides a scaffold because they have a framework for how the words are grouped (e.g., social studies words, math words, science words, etc.). Depending on the purpose of the activity, level of students, and their familiarity with the activity, teachers can determine which kind of sort is most effective for meeting their instructional goals. If students are new to sorting, a closed sort makes sense. Because Sandy knew the students were familiar with sorting, and because she wanted them to preview their content area textbooks, she created an open concept sort using a sheet of words like those in Figure 6.1.

Students are put into groups, given the word sheet, and asked to cut out the words and arrange them into groups that make sense to them. After they finish sorting, each group explains how they sorted the words and their reasons for doing so. Through the discussion that follows, students get a heads-up on the topics and

prairie	rectangle	citizen
tribe	biotic	remainder
ecosystem	array	habitat
odd number	abiotic	heritage
artifact	society	even number
quotient	prime number	scale

FIGURE 6.1. Concept Sort.

associated vocabulary that they will be studying in each of the disciplines in the upcoming weeks. For more information on word sorts, see *Words Their Way 4th Edition* (Bear, Invernizzi, Templeton, & Johnston, 2007).

Word Think Sheets

As we described in Chapter 1, Carole's planning sometimes includes preteaching upcoming math words in vocabulary instruction. She also plans to provide her third graders with the routines of a "workshop" format that include a mini-lesson, guided practice, and independent practice. Carole has developed a Word Think Sheet to help students structure the process of thinking and learning about words. The Word Think Sheet is a variation of the Frayer Model (Frayer, Frederick, & Klausmeier, 1969). In the Frayer Model, a sheet of paper is divided into four quadrants with the term for study in the middle of the page. In the first quadrant, students are directed to provide a definition of the word. In the second quadrant, students list all of the facts that they know about the word. In the third and fourth quadrants, students list examples and nonexamples of the term. Carole modified the sheet for mathematics vocabulary and to address the developmental level of her students. Figure 6.2 shows a blank version of the sheet Carole used. The math term is placed at the top of the sheet. In the first quadrant, students are to draw a picture representing the term. The second quadrant asks students to make connections to other related words they might know. The third quadrant asks for the term to be used in a sentence. Finally, in the fourth quadrant, students are to suggest a definition or meaning for the term.

Before giving the children the Word Think Sheet, Carole models sketching pictures about a few words (mini-lesson) and then invites the children to draw their own sketches in their notebooks (guided practice). Over time, she models thinking of other related words and using the math word in a sentence while students practice. Finally they work on the challenging task of trying to express the meaning of the word. This does not have to be a perfect definition, especially for a concept that third graders are still building. Carole encourages children to express their current understanding of the word in a definition-like format. After several demonstrations of all four quadrants and practice by students in their notebooks, Carole introduces the Word Think Sheet. She can then show them how all of the quadrants help them learn about the new term. Eventually, when it is clear that the children have become familiar with the Word Think Sheet and know how to use it, she asks them to apply their knowledge in independent practice. During reading and writing workshops, the Word Think Sheet becomes a tool they use independently to show their thinking about words from the week's mathematics vocabulary list. After an independent work session, the class is reconvened to reflect and to share their work.

Over time, Carole will teach them more about writing definitions. Later in the year, after they know the words well, students will look up definitions in the glos-

Name _____ Date _____

Word	
Picture	Other words it makes me think of:
Good sentence	Meaning

FIGURE 6.2. Word Think Sheet.

From *Integrating Literacy and Math: Strategies for K–6 Teachers* by Ellen Fogelberg, Carole Skalinder, Patti Satz, Barbara Hiller, Lisa Bernstein, and Sandra Vitantonio. Copyright 2008 by The Guilford Press. Permission to photocopy this figure is granted to purchasers of this book for personal use only (see copyright page for details).

sary of the math text and compare the more formal definitions with their own definitions. Using dictionaries and glossaries in this fashion is another hallmark of effective vocabulary instruction. This framework for using the Word Think Sheet is summarized in Figure 6.3.

Carole's class had been struggling to generate number sentences to represent a series of statements: What number is 16 more than 20? What number is 8 more than 17? What number is 30 more than 100? It was difficult for everyone to understand the phrase, "16 *more than* 20." Later that day, in Word Study time, Carole asked the children to draw sketches to represent the word *difference*. Jackie giggled as she drew a girl with blond hair next to a girl with dark hair. That gave Carole an opportunity to talk with the class about the interesting layers of "ordinary meanings" and "math meanings" associated with many words. The class became quiet and focused. The idea resonated with them.

---

1. Introduce the math word or concept in a mini-lesson.
   - The teacher thinks aloud and demonstrates how to make a sketch (first quadrant) showing understandings about the word ("math meaning" or "ordinary meaning").
   - The mini-lesson may include discussions as children begin to put together their thoughts and build understanding.

2. Provide guided practice.
   - Circulate and assist children as they create drawings to illustrate the word.
   - Monitor and facilitate conversations.

3. Continue mini-lessons and guided practice for each box on the think sheet until children are proficient.

4. Help children make connections.
   - Refer to student ideas during discussions of the same concept in math lessons.
   - Refer to the same word or concept while reading related texts.

5. Provide opportunities for children to practice independently.
   - Students choose one or two words from the word wall or spelling list.
   - Students complete think sheets for their chosen words.

6. Reconvene briefly after independent practice. Allow the class to share their thinking.

FIGURE 6.3. Framework for using a Word Think Sheet.

Carole decided to begin the following day's math instruction by exploring the children's conceptions of the "ordinary" meaning of the word *difference,* and then asked them to make connections to deepen their understanding of the "math" uses of the word. She did this with guided practice on the Word Think Sheet. The children wrote the word "difference" at the top of their sheet. She then asked students to discuss the word informally with their partners. After circulating and assisting, Carole asked them to individually sketch a picture of what the word *difference* means and to write the meaning of the word. Most of the students wrote about the "ordinary" meaning of *difference*:

"Boys are smellier than girls. That's why they are so different."
"The difference between a cat and a dog is their height."
"Difference means things are not the same."

In the next few days, math lessons referred to "finding differences." Carole asked for examples from their work on the think sheets. The children quickly referred to their previous thinking. She had not yet asked them to fill in the quadrant for words related to the target word or the quadrants to use the word in a sentence.

Terry: "These two things are not quite the same (referring to a drawing of a little dog next to a bigger dog). They are a little bit *different.*

Carole reminded the students about the words "16 more than 20." She said, "This dog's height is not the same as the other dog's height. Its height is *more than* that one's height. There is a difference. What we want to know is how much more is it? How much *difference* is there?"

The class also had opportunities to make connections in their reading. Several books in the classroom referred to the concept of "difference," either explicitly or implicitly. Using the book *Numbers and You* (O'Sullivan, 2004a) students in a guided reading group read a caption about a baby's body having more bones than an adult's body. With Carole's help, the group wrote a subtraction problem comparing the two, using the word "difference."

Because of their extended opportunities to talk about, draw, and define the word *difference* students now understood enough about the concept to complete the remaining quadrants on the Word Think Sheet. They returned to the question, "What number is 16 more than 20?" and could then translate the words into a number sentence: _?_ = 20 + 16.

Starting with Student Language

Preparing to create a think sheet on the word *digit,* Carole asked the class if they knew anything about the word *digit.* They did not have much to say, so she asked if anyone knew one little thing? Had they ever heard the word? Did they have any associations? She called on all the children one at a time for each to say what they knew or associated with the word.

"2 is a digit."
"You can move them around."
"A digit can be like 2, 3, 4."
"A digit can be a number."
"A negative number can be a digit."
"A digit can be odd or even."
"A number by itself."
"A digit is a number that makes other numbers."
"Digits are everywhere in the world."
"A digit can be in any number."
"Only numbers are digits."
"5,000 would be 4 digits."
"38 is a 2-digit number."
"I don't know."
"A digit is a number."
"A digit is a code."
"A digit is a single number that is alone and doesn't have another number with it."

The last child happened to be a fragile math student, targeted by the school for close monitoring of her achievement. By the time her turn came, she was able to piece together all of the class's thoughts to come up with a pretty good description of what a digit is. Certainly the class had constructed a good picture of the concept of "digit."

Introducing the Math Concept before Introducing the Term

Following the curriculum, Carole planned to teach a third-grade unit on area and perimeter. In the past, students seemed to understand area and perimeter for the duration of the unit, but became confused about the terms when presented with problems on the state test in spring. This year she decided to get the students to use and name the concept of "area" before giving them the labels. The lesson as designed in the Everyday Math program began with a problem that asks students to find out how many 1-foot squares it takes to cover a larger square, 1 yard on each side. Students worked on the problem in small groups, measuring, cutting, and covering the larger square with smaller ones. Carole had prepared a chart called, "Invented Words" headed: "The number of small squares it takes to cover the big square is called the . . . " Adams (2003, p. 787) states, "It is acceptable for students to use informal definitions as an introduction to formal definitions." The idea was to get students engaged as quickly as possible in thinking of these names to make the connection more powerful when they need the mathematical word. Carole had to accomplish this quickly because the word *area* was on the next day's homework.

Each student group had solved the initial area problem in a slightly different way. One group placed three small squares at the bottom of the large square and then figured out that two more rows of three would fill it. Another group had simply drawn a grid of 1-foot squares on the large square. Another group actually cut out nine small squares and taped them on the larger square. One group had encountered trouble cutting out the smaller squares, and ended up arranging smaller pieces in an unusual way.

Because there were so many variations, Carole thought that it would be interesting to have each group make a brief presentation of how they had worked it out. She also asked each group to commit to a name for "how many squares it takes to cover up the larger square." (If their solutions had all been the same, this option would have been meaningless.) After a break, Carole read a little book called *Baby Bear Quilt* (Irons, 1993) about a bear making a quilt—it was a perfect fit for this situation. The students then made their presentations and together the class created a list of words to describe what they were finding out: "squares in the shape," "quilt squares," and "bed-covering size."

At the beginning of the next day's lesson, Carole introduced the next problem in the lesson for discussion: She asked students to figure out how many 1-yard squares it takes to cover the classroom floor, as if they were buying a new carpet for the class. They reviewed the invented terms and discovered that it was awkward trying to apply their invented terms to what they were currently doing. So, Carole asked them if they have ever heard of a word that means what they were doing. Some students remembered that the process is referred to as finding area. The class then began using the word *area* to talk about what they were doing. Carole thinks that this exercise may help the word stick to the concept more effectively. At the very least, the students have the experience to refer to when trying to remember what area means.

Metaphors

The discussion above demonstrates another important facet of mathematical vocabulary learning. The children use metaphors to describe a process or concept. Finding the area is described as the process of figuring out "bed-covering size," and a digit is described as a code. Whitin and Whitin (2000) suggest that metaphors allow children to be risk takers and that the metaphors they develop reflect their individuality. We have found that children use metaphors in their everyday language as they grapple with new ideas and concepts. The metaphors help create a rich supply of images to draw upon as their emerging understandings of new concepts develop. For example, when Patti's second-grade class started using multiplication number models, they realized that they needed to distinguish between the different numbers in the sentence: those that were multiplied together and those that represented the answer. Instead of telling her class the formal names of "factor" and "product," Patti asked her students what they thought would be good names for these pieces of the number model based on the function of the piece. Students suggested *math, magic,* and *mul* as possibilities for the factors and *summary* and *plication* for the product. They became so engaged and felt so empowered to be able to give a name to a math concept that they even created a ballot and voted for their favorite terms. Within a week the students understood the function of the parts and were ready for the terms *factor* and *product.* Working through the multiplication models using their own language created the condition for students to want to use the correct terminology to communicate effectively and precisely with others about the process used to solve multiplication problems.

How the Little Words Cause Big Confusions

Because mathematics includes using familiar words in unfamiliar ways, context is not always helpful, especially for non-native speakers. Kenney (2005, p. 7) sums up the difficulties nicely: "In mathematics, vocabulary may be confusing because the words mean different things in mathematics and nonmathematics context, because two different words sound the same, or because more than one word is used to describe the same concept."

Using the notetaking strategy for problem solving described in Chapter 4 and a think-aloud, Patti helped her second graders work through the following problem highlighting the "tricky" math words.

> There are a total of 23 books on two shelves in Jason's room. When he takes away 8 books on the first shelf, there are 5 books left on it. How many books are on the second shelf?

Patti read the problem with the students, asked them to work out the problem by themselves and then, working as a class, they made a list of the math words used in the problem. They came up with the following word list:

> total (or sum), 23 books on two shelves, take away 8 books, 5 left on the first shelf, how many books are on the second shelf?

Students struggled with the concept of "left on the shelf." To help them distinguish between the common meaning of *left* (the opposite of right) and the mathematical meaning (remains), Patti thought aloud about the way the author stated the problem.

> "I'm thinking about the sentence, when he takes away 8 books on the first shelf, there are 5 books left on it. I know the word *left.* It means the opposite

of right, like my left side is the opposite of my right side. And, I know that when I make a left turn, it is the opposite of a right turn. I don't think that makes sense in this sentence. I also know that when I am playing cards and there are no cards left, the game is over. When I think of left in that way, it means that no cards remain in the pile. Maybe left means remain. I'll try that in the sentence instead of left. When I take away 8 books on the first shelf, there are 5 books remaining. That makes sense to me."

Patti demonstrated how to connect the ordinary meaning of the word to the mathematical meaning as used in the problem.

Then, with Patti's help, students restated the problem to say, "Take away 8 books, so that 5 remain on the first shelf." Based on this discussion, the class decided that they needed to find the total of the first shelf to find what remained on the second shelf. Patti added the word *left* to the class list of words that mean something different when used in math.

Because students pulled apart the problem to list the math words, they quickly got to the confusing part, the use of the word *left*, took care of it, and could then move on to get to the essence of the problem. In the next example, the tricky words were *all* and *an* from the following problem:

> Six adults and 9 children were going to see a movie. An adult ticket cost $5.00 and the child's ticket cost $1.50. How much did all of the tickets for the movie cost?

The class discussion turned toward the word *all*. The children, again with Patti's help, decided that *all* meant "total." Next, they discussed *an* as in "an adult." They decided that *an* meant "one." They had to restate the problem several times. Some students did not make the connection that there were 6 adults and 9 children and that each one needed to pay. Some students decided the answer was $6.50. Patti asked students to role play buying tickets so they could imagine 6 adults and 9 children buying the tickets. Although most students understood what the problem was asking, some were unable to reason through it because they did not understand the role of the "little" words *all* and *an* in the context of the problem. Rereading did not provide enough support to figure out the problem. Patti realized that students needed additional help before they could paraphrase the problem. Kenney (2005, p. 15) states, "Enunciating small but significant words more precisely, being more aware of the confusion that these words can engender, and emphasizing the correct use of these little land mines will not only enhance computational skills, but also help students answer open-response questions more accurately."

As students progress through the elementary grades, they are expected to read and comprehend mathematical problems in the context of a story or as posed in the context of a real-life situation. Words that have multiple meanings may present problems to the reading comprehension of the situation as illustrated above. Other examples include the word *volume*, which has the mathematical meaning of "space taken up by an object," but the everyday meaning of "noise level," and the word *yard*, which means "3 feet" in a math context, but can also mean "a grassy area around a building." To have some fun with this and to make students aware of multiple meanings, Sandy suggests that students keep and post on the wall a list of common words that also have different, but specific meanings when used in math. To increase enjoyment of the activity, Sandy invites the students' families to contribute words to the display at curriculum night and when they come to conferences.

Homophones

The many homophones that students encounter in math class also present challenges. Words such as *some*, *ate*, and *way* are words used in everyday language that sound the same as the common math words *sum*, *eight*, and *weigh*. Read *Eight Ate: A Feast of Homonym Riddles* (Terban, 1986) to get students excited about looking for homophones to add to a class-generated list. Figure 6.4 shows a partial list of confusing homophones.

English language learners (ELLs) often have greater difficulty with homophones and multiple meaning words because the various meanings are often represented by more than one word in the first language. Olivares (1996, p. 222) gives the example of the word *table*, " . . . in Spanish the equivalent for *table* (furniture) is *mesa*. The equivalent for the mathematical meaning of *table* is *tabla*. However, *tabla* in Spanish also means *board* and not furniture. Transference could work for the concept but not always for the terminology." The activities suggested throughout this chapter support second language learners. However, teachers must be aware of the additional difficulty that ELL students may experience with multiple meaning words.

Homophones	
Cent	Sent or scent
Sum	Some
Whole	Hole
One	Won
Plane	Plain

FIGURE 6.4. Anchor chart: Homophones.

MODELS OF WORD LEARNING BEHAVIORS

Vocabulary Notebooks

Some of our fifth-grade students keep academic vocabulary notebooks. After working with the vocabulary of a particular unit, they proceed to create an entry in their notebook. Sandy expects students to describe the term in their own words and to provide a sketch or example of the word. Whitin and Whitin (2000, p. 78) suggest that by using their own language in developing a definition, "students place a unique personal signature on each of their definitions and often include attributes that textbooks leave out." Influenced by Marzano's (2004) work, the teachers ask the students to come back to the entry later in the unit to add to their growing definition and to adjust and add to their sketches. By reviewing the notebooks, the teachers quickly assess student understanding of the vocabulary words and may revise their lessons if further teaching is warranted. Students use the notebooks to quiz each other and refer to them often. Once the entry is included in the notebook, teachers expect students to use the term in discussion and writing.

Categorizing Math Words by Parts of Speech

Students in the intermediate grades keep a manila folder with the following categories listed at the top of each: "Nouns, "Verbs," "Adjectives," and "Adverbs." Students begin to understand that they think about words differently based on the part of speech, another aspect of vocabulary instruction (Marzano, 2004). By categorizing the mathematical terms by part of speech, students also learn more about the process and content of mathematics: some words are verbs and convey action; others are nouns and are usually acted upon; others can be changed by adding a suffix to serve as adjectives (e.g., digital clock, rectangular surface, etc.). Finally, students have the words readily available for use in their writing. The words remain on the class math content word wall all year.

By adding the part of speech, we are helping students develop and expand their "working" definition of the words. Ball and Bass (2001, p. 30) eloquently describe the process of learning about words and coming to a definition: "Definitions are not simply delivered names to be memorized. They are seeded or conceived in concepts; they gestate through active investigation and reflection, and when they come to term, they are born out of a need to describe a rich or important idea in need of easy reference to facilitate its entry into common discourse." Murray (2004) suggests that the students' accurate use of vocabulary is an effective measure of conceptual understanding. So, we listen in to students' discussion as they work collaboratively to solve problems and use operations to explain their thinking, noting their use of mathematical vocabulary. We use anecdotal records to keep track of the language students are using in order to monitor their conceptual understanding and to inform our teaching. We keep trying, in developmentally appropriate ways, to move students through the process described above by Ball and Bass.

With respect to morphology, Graves (2006) suggests that primary teachers use short and informal mini-lessons for teaching word parts. By fourth grade, teachers can begin formally teaching word parts in combination with context clues. We teach word parts in mathematics class by explaining how endings may change the part of speech (e.g., rectangular prism) and helping students understand the meaning of the new word. We are primarily concerned with teaching the mathematical terms that are important to the unit of study and those that the students are ready to use because they have some understanding of the concepts behind the terms.

Word Grid

When children are ready to use a more sophisticated think sheet, Carole repeats the same steps as in the Word Think Sheet (Figure 6.2) framework with a graphic organizer she has labeled "Advanced Word Think Sheet." The vocabulary term appears in the first of nine boxes. These include the original four quadrants that request a picture, related words, a sentence, and a meaning. In addition, because the students have begun working with categorizing the math words by part of speech, Carole asks them to identify the part of speech and root word, and to break the word into syllables. Figure 6.5 shows a sample Advanced Word Think Sheet as completed by a third-grade student for the term *tenths*. The Word Think Sheet can be pasted into the vocabulary notebook for easy reference.

Concept Definition Map

Through the use of scaffolds like the Word Think Sheet and the Word Grid, students in Carole's class gradually develop the idea of putting all the information they have about the words into a definition-like format. At this point, Carole decides to introduce them to a "Concept Definition Map" for the concept of area. In the past, Carole had worked with third-grade students to develop concept maps of science and social studies vocabulary. She is hoping that using the map for area and perimeter will help solidify the concepts for the students.

A Concept Definition Map (Schwartz & Raphael, 1985) helps students organize the information they have about a word by categorizing it and including semantic information along with examples and nonexamples. While this type of mapping is typically used with older students, Carole found it effective and after modeling the process and giving lots of practice, students enjoyed using it to create definitions for words used in all of the content areas. Using maps created by students from previous classes as exemplars, Carole cocreated one with the students for area, as shown in Figure 6.6.

Name _____

Write the word *tenths*	Other words it reminds me of *tenth thousands* *fraction*	Use the word in a sentence *You can put ten* *tenths* *in a circle.*
Draw a picture showing the meaning *one* *tenth*	What the word means *Some thing is* *divided into ten* *pieces.* *Tenths.*	Example *Each pkg of gum* *is one tenth* *because there are* *ten in a big* *packig.*
Part of speech *noun*	Show the word divided into syllables *tenths*	Root or base word *ten*

FIGURE 6.5. Advanced Word Think Sheet for the term *tenths*.

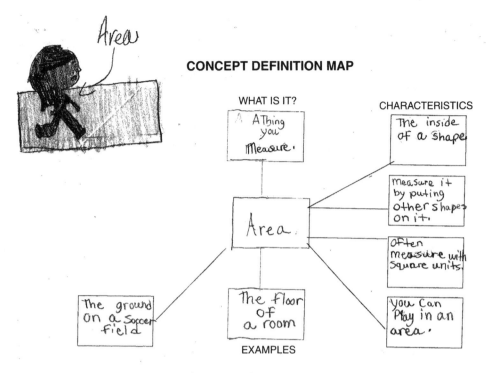

FIGURE 6.6. Concept Definition Map of *area.*

To begin, teachers model the process all the way through so that students understand the purpose of the map and know how to fill in the parts. In this example, Carole put the word *area* in the center of the map that she had put onto an overhead transparency. The students had a copy of the blank map to use as they worked through the process as a class. She then asked students to think about the broader category of mathematics that they were studying. The class quickly named the unit from the math series, measurement, and placed the topic in the square above the word area. This is an important part of the process; students need to see how this topic fits into the mathematics they are studying, as well as to think about how and why one calculates area. Carole then directed students to think about the characteristics of area. "What is area and how do we figure it out?" was the language she used to help them understand what is meant by characteristics. To further scaffold, Carole asked students to draw an example of what it looks like when someone is determining the area of a surface. Students used the blank area of the map to draw a representation of finding area. Once the representations were completed, Carole and the students quickly filled in the sections under characteristics, stating that *area* is "the inside of a shape," and that you, "measure it by putting other shapes on it," and that you "often measure [it] with square units," and finally, "that you can play in an area."

The next section of the map, "examples," is relatively easy to fill in once students have categorized the word and determined its characteristics. Students suggested the ground on a soccer field and the floor of a room as examples of when one wants to find out area. Finally, Carole showed the students that one can use the information in the Concept Definition Map to write a dictionary-like definition. Together, they crafted a definition that they were all satisfied with: Area is a thing you measure. It is the inside of a shape. You measure it by putting other shapes on it, often squares. Examples: We can find the area of the ground of a soccer field, the floor of a room, and of our orange square rug.

Games: "I Have, Who Has?"

Our math program includes the use of games to reinforce basic math facts and to practice other math skills. Observing students as they play the games provides teachers with a quick assessment of students' current facility in using math facts and creates a window into their development of other skills. Carole, after reading about the game, "I Have, Who Has?" (Association of Teachers of Mathematics in Maine Newsletter, Winter 2000) in several different professional books, decided to add it to the third-grade cache of games. Carole created a set of cards for the words under study as shown in Figure 6.7 with a vocabulary term on the front, and a definition for a different word on the back. The game is played as follows: The teacher creates a sheet with several words in boxes. He or she then cuts the words apart and tapes each one on the front of a card under the heading, "I have . . . " A definition for another word goes on the back of each card under the heading, "Who has . . . ?" The teacher then distributes the words and definitions to the students. He or she starts by saying, "Who has _____?" and reads the definition on the back of one card. Students must listen to the definition and decide if it matches the word on the front of one of their cards. If it matches, that student says, "I have _____." The same student then repeats the process saying, "Who has _____?" and reads the definition on his or her card. Sometimes, the game continues until all the cards are used and the last person answers, "I have _____." Initially, however, Carole chooses just a few of the cards so that the students get used to the game and can learn to play it rather quickly.

Carole's students love the game. They practice reading the definitions to make sure they are prepared when it is their turn. They also work with partners to check the answers to the definition questions. This allows for repeated exposure to new terms and creates an opportunity to revisit words even after a unit of study is com-

The total when two or more numbers are added	sum	Shapes or numbers that repeat in a regular way
The amount of time that has gone by	elapsed time	pattern
Going backwards	reverse	Every one
Numbers can be added or multiplied in either order.	turn-around facts	each
An answer that is figured out to be close, but not exact	estimate	The amount by which one number is greater or less than another number
Find out if two things are alike or different.	compare	difference
A number sentence or equation used to solve a problem	number model	Objects in rows and columns
"For each" or "in each"	per	array

FIGURE 6.7. Word template for the "I Have, Who Has?" game (*page 1 of 2*).

The result of multiplication	product	A rectangle whose sides are each one foot long
The distance around a shape	perimeter	square foot
Measurement of the space on a surface	area	The distance around the outside of a circle
The figures 0, 1, 2, 3, 4, 5, 6, 7, 8, 9	digits	circumference
A particular face on a 3-dimensional shape	base	One of the flat surfaces on a 3-dimensional figure
A point where the sides of a polygon meet	vertex	face
A border where the surfaces of a 3-dimensional shape meet	edge	Extending in the same direction but never meeting
Numbers that are multiplied together to get a product	factors	parallel

FIGURE 6.7. *(page 2 of 2)*

pleted. Murray (2004) cites Willingham's (2002) research on the effects of distributive or spaced practice on memory as being superior to studying something for a single time frame.

Support for ELLs

ELLs must learn the same mathematics as their English-speaking peers. However, ELL students have to learn to think mathematically and develop problem-solving strategies in a second language. According to Olivares (1996, p. 220), "Communicative competence in the language of mathematics is a necessary condition for mathematics learning." While many terms for mathematics can be transferred from one language to another (e.g., for native Spanish speakers, *digits* are *digitos*), second language learners often experience comprehension difficulties with word problems because of multiple meaning words and common words that are often used in conversation but have a different meaning when used in mathematics. They cannot use context to figure out what they are supposed to do to solve a problem. Olivares suggests that students use visualizing, drawing, manipulatives, and dramatizing as ways to represent what they think the problem is about.

Olivares also suggests that teachers allow ELL students to use their first language to talk about problems and make sense of the mathematics. However, Olivares (1996, p. 229) goes on to say that ELLs will "continue to be mathematically limited in their new language until they are able to achieve mathematical language proficiency in English." Therefore, he recommends that ELL students be exposed to a learning environment that focuses on mathematical communication in the second language. Our bilingual Spanish teachers present mathematics in the student's first language until about the middle of third grade. They then move to providing support in English using cognates and anchor charts. The timing seems appropriate as it is in third grade that many mathematical terms are used to describe more sophisticated concepts.

Final Thoughts

The guidelines for effective vocabulary instruction developed by Blachowicz and Fisher (2002) provide the basic framework for how we organize our vocabulary instruction in all content areas. It is especially helpful for thinking about teaching the language of mathematics because it addresses a variety of our concerns about how to support our students as they learn to communicate mathematically. Immersing the students in the language, teaching strategies and word-learning behaviors that lead to independent learning, and using assessments that match the goals of instruction help us address the NCTM Principles (2000) for teaching and learning.

Our job is to determine the common knowledge students bring to the content, to activate this knowledge, and to create opportunities to develop new knowledge. We believe that working with the vocabulary is one way to bring in new knowledge and to enhance the background knowledge students already have. The lessons we share in this chapter are all designed to uncover what students know about particular mathematical concepts and words, and to then extend that knowledge to increase students' ability to use the language of mathematics to solve problems (both inside and outside of school), and to help them make sense of their world.

CHAPTER 7
MATH WRITING

Counting by fours
Adding cats and hats together
Subtracting bones from dogs
Doubling numbers large and small
Measuring the length of Asia
Multiplying pairs of shoes
Dividing pencils into groups
Erasing mistakes
No problem!

—Poem on -*ing*
by a second-grade class

Communication is an important process standard recorded in the NCTM *Principles and Standards for School Mathematics* (2000) and writing, as a form of communication, has become an important part of our work. In this chapter we will concentrate on mathematical writing, a tool that provides the teacher with a way to look at individual student strategies and understanding while encouraging students to reflect and revise their thinking.

Murray (2004, pp. 88–89) has identified several benefits to having students write about the mathematics that they are doing:

➢ Thoughtfulness and increased reasoning skills
➢ Active involvement in thinking and making sense, constructing and learning mathematics
➢ Questions raised and new ideas explored
➢ Use of higher-order thinking while interpreting and explaining data
➢ Clarification, reinforcement, and deepened conceptual understanding

➤ Teacher insights:
   student thinking revealed
   understanding verified or misconceptions uncovered
   student attitudes and needs identified
   communication between teacher and individual student

➤ Self-reflection and self-directed learning
   awareness of what they know, do not know, and need to know
   awareness of what they can do, cannot do, and need to learn how to do

We let students know that we expect them to write in math class for a variety of reasons: to assess their understanding, to record their thinking in order to revise their approach at a later time, to share problem-solving strategies with their peers and teacher, and to share feelings and frustrations about the mathematics they are studying. If students are to take a risk in their writing, then we must be patient, encouraging, and supportive. When our students write about their understanding of and approaches to a solution, it validates what we have been saying to them—that there are many approaches to mathematical problem solving and that their thinking is important.

As we've seen in the previous chapters, students begin problem solving or the study of math vocabulary by creating drawings or sketches. Students can adjust their drawings as their understanding of a concept changes. Writing—including drawing and diagramming—provides an opportunity for a teacher to see students' thinking, their questions, their use of mathematical vocabulary, and their understanding of previously taught math topics. In many students' writings we see their organization of thought and even the "aha!" moment of understanding. In one case, a fifth-grade student realized that use of the number line not only made her solution explainable but led to the "assumptions" (student's word) that allowed her to understand and visualize her solution. "I realized," "probably will," and "information from the diagram showed" were expressions that she used in writing her conclusions. While other students may not always be as sophisticated in their writing, the process of expressing their thinking helps clarify their understanding of the problem and its solution.

Teachers use student writings and skills to determine whether to reteach a concept or to continue more in-depth understanding. We value the use of student errors to reteach and help students rethink and justify their work.

WRITING FOR PROBLEM SOLVING

"Explanations that are simply procedural descriptions or summaries should give way to mathematical arguments." (*Principles and Standards for School Mathematics*, 2000, p. 186). "The solution of mathematical word problems depends on two sets of knowledge—linguistic knowledge and symbolic/mathematical knowledge" (Pape, 2004, p. 190). All students in a class must be able to think, talk, and write about a chosen problem.

In Illinois we are guided by the Illinois Standards Achievement Test (ISAT). The state provides a rubric for writing about mathematics problem solving. (For those who might be interested, the "student-friendly" Mathematics Scoring Rubric may be found at *www.isbe.net/assessment/math.htm.*) Using this rubric, we teach students to develop three main competencies when writing about their problem solving: (1) mathematical knowledge, or "getting the right answer," (2) strategic knowledge, or "showing all the steps," and (3) explanation, or writing "*what* I did and "*why* I did it." Our teaching has evolved as we have found ways to communicate these processes to children. For example, think sheets such as those described in this chapter are used to scaffold the process for explaining.

Students' writing allows us to see their initial mathematical understanding and their growth as they are encouraged to explore, talk, and write. As students' understanding grows, there is visible, progressive change in their approach to writing and solving problems.

Carole's initial writing task for her third graders was a sheet with the following problem:

> Lia had 182 pennies in a cup. She spent 94 of them on a goldfish. How many pennies does she have left in the cup?

On the sheet in two separate boxes, students were asked to first show what this problem looked like and then what their solution looked like. Figure 7.1 shows Rey's completed worksheet. He uses a simple picture labeled with words to take apart the problem. Numbers and words show his understanding of the question and solution. The worksheet of another student, Litza, can be seen in Figure 7.2. She uses a more detailed picture, using only two words, "Friday" and "Saturday," to show the meaning of the problem. Litza's solution is arithmetical using a single word, "pennies," to label the answer. The work of both students shows how they understand the written problem and their solution process. The importance of this work is not the answer to the problem: their thinking process is made visible.

By January, Rey's much more detailed approach to a posed problem shows the result of carefully scaffolded work over a 4-week period of time. As seen in Figure 7.3, the solution shows a clear understanding of the question and a very detailed arithmetical solution that shows his thinking process. Four additional questions have been added to this think sheet. These ask students to describe in words what they have shown in the two boxes: "What I drew to show the problem," "Why I drew that," "What I drew to show the solution," and "Why I drew that." Rey's answers to these questions are a descriptive listing of the steps he followed to arrive at a solution. They can be seen in Figures 7.4 and 7.5.

Lia had 182 pennies in a cup. She
spent 94 of them on a goldfish. How
many pennies does she have left in
the cup?

What the problem looks like:

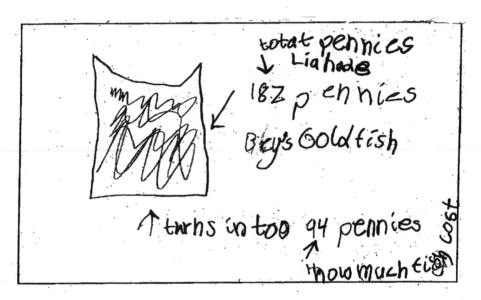

What the solution looks like:

FIGURE 7.1. Rey's initial worksheet, from early December.

FIGURE 7.2. Litza's December worksheet.

Name _____

> Emily had some stickers. Sean gave her 18 more stickers. Now she has 32. How many stickers did Emily have to begin with?

What the problem looks like:

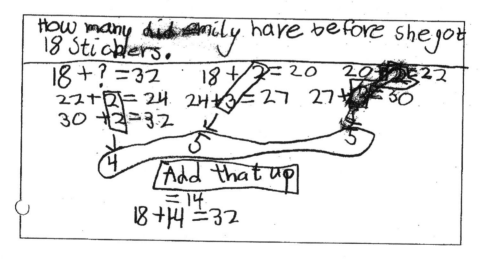

Emily has some do not now now many stickeres she has.

Emily
? Stickeres

Sean gave 18 stickers to Emily

What the solution looks like:

How many did emily have before she got 18 Stichers.

18 + ? = 32   18 + ? = 20   20 + ? = 22
22 + ? = 24   24 + ? = 27   27 + ? = 30
30 + ? = 32   5   5
   4

Add that up
          = 14
18 + 14 = 32

FIGURE 7.3. Rey's January worksheet, part I.

Name_____Date_____

What I drew to show the problem	Why I drew that
First I drew a Box that said Emily on it, that had ? for stickers	Because we do not now how many stickers she has.
Then Sean gave Emily 18 stickers.	Be cause Sean gave Emily 18 more stickers.

FIGURE 7.4. Rey's January worksheet, part II.

Name_____Date_____

What I drew to show the solution	Why I drew that
Frist I put a number moldel had 18 + ? = 32. Then I plased by 3 and by 2 from 18. too 32. Then I got all the 3's and the 2's out of the stuff I piased and got, 4, 5. itup and then Padded number was 14 stickers.	Becaduse that how many stickers we now she has An we now she has 32 Stickers. Because too find Out how many sticker she had in the tdjing. Be cause those were the answer numbers. Because to find Out the answer.

FIGURE 7.5. Rey's January worksheet, part III.

As illustrated by Rey's worksheets, student problem-solving writing begins to look like the level of work required for the state tests. In Rey's January worksheets, a more sophisticated level of the written explanation is seen. The arithmetic solutions (using addition and subtraction) are similar but the written explanation has become clearer as he identifies specific steps in the working process followed by a concluding sentence that answers the question.

Another student, Paul, described his solution to a similar problem. His written explanation is seen in Figure 7.6. Using words like "I know," "first," and "next," Paul makes his explanation easy to follow to his conclusion. The drawings and

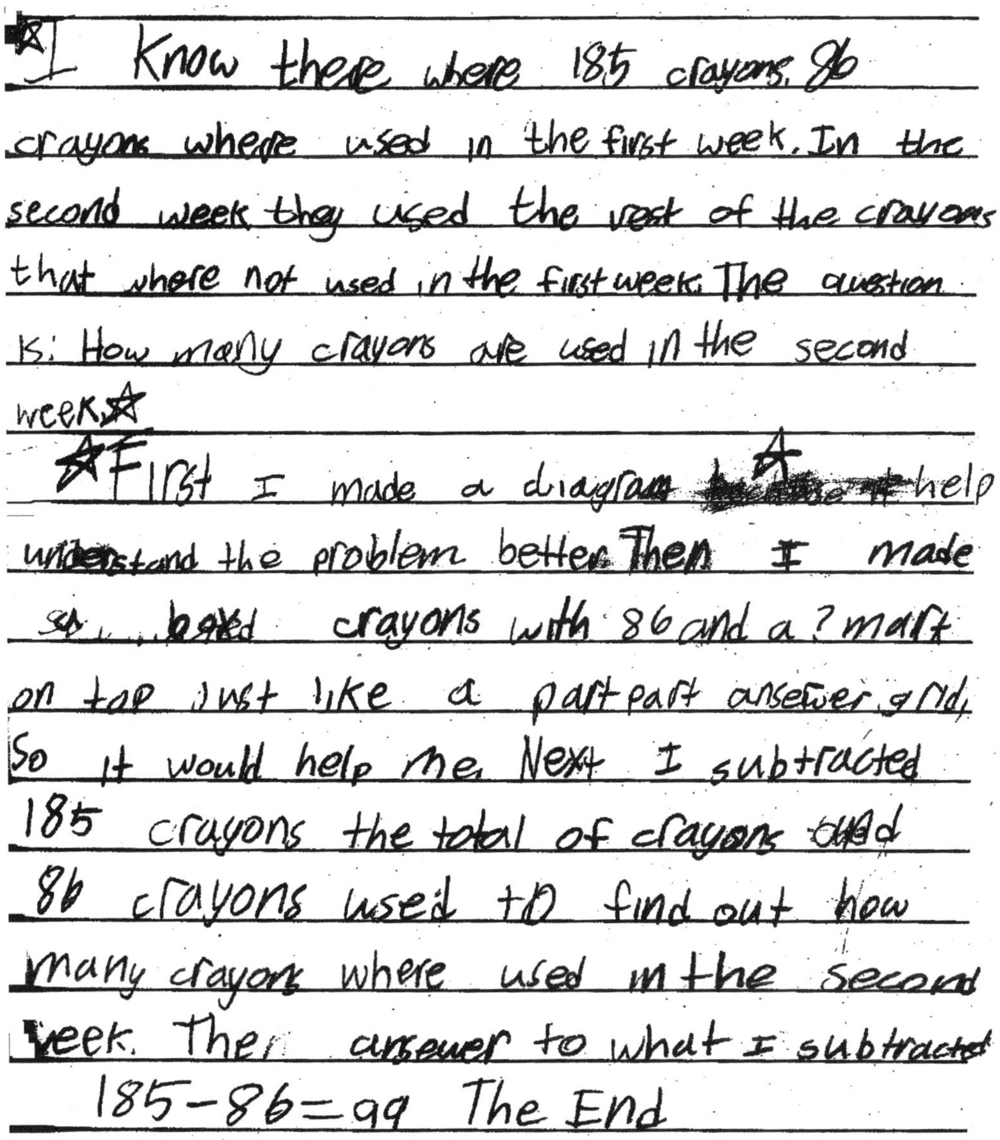

⭐I know there where 185 crayons. 86 crayons where used in the first week. In the second week they used the rest of the crayons that where not used in the first week. The question is: How many crayons are used in the second week.⭐

⭐First I made a diagram ~~to the help~~ help understand the problem better. Then I made so, boxed crayons with 86 and a ? mart on top just like a part part ansewer. and, so it would help me. Next I subtracted 185 crayons the total of crayons ~~old~~ 86 crayons used to find out how many crayon where used in the second week. Then ansewer to what I subtracted 185−86=99 The End

FIGURE 7.6. Paul's explanation.

written descriptions of "What the problem looks like" are written elaborately by some students and very simply by others; either way it shows the students' thinking as they read the problem. These drawings are a way of paraphrasing and a way of leading students to rewrite the problem in their own words. Explaining their work also allows students to self-check (Does it make sense?), adjusting their approach if necessary. The ultimate goal is to have students write a clear analysis of their problem solving by justifying their work and using mathematical vocabulary.

USING MATH WRITING AS A STUDENT CONFERENCING TOOL

When we find opportunities to conference with students who struggle, we are often limited in the amount of time we can spend in each conference. Having samples of the student's writing on hand helps us to focus our conferencing on one issue at a time. We can then make good choices about which aspect of the student's thinking process to address during the conference.

Odessa is a third-grade math student who is just developing number sense. Carole wants to help her use real-world contexts to understand the concept of comparing numbers. To do so Carole uses the think sheet that Odessa has completed about the following problem:

> A peddler had 37 caps on his head when the day started. During the day some monkeys stole some of his caps. When he came home he had 12 caps. How many caps did the monkeys steal?

Odessa has restated the question nicely but instead of restating the pieces of information separately on the think sheet, she has restated the entire problem. Her drawings show wonderful illustrations of the story with monkeys and a sleeping peddler. But she does not indicate the number of hats in the picture. At the end of the paper, where Odessa is asked, "What did you find out?" she writes, "I found out that 37—25 = 12." While the computation is correct, this number statement has no context.

In the conference with Odessa, Carole decides to build on a strength in her work: the ability to paraphrase the question clearly. She is trying to find out how many caps the monkeys took. Carole wants to get Odessa to relate her computation to the context of the question.

CAROLE: What were you supposed to try to find out?

ODESSA: We want to find out how many hats did the monkeys take.

CAROLE: Right. So . . . I see that you subtracted 25 from 37. That was right. Why did you do that? What were you finding out?

ODESSA: I was finding out how many hats the monkeys took.

CAROLE: So . . . how could you write that in this box?

ODESSA: They stole 12 hats.

Carole next works with Odessa to paraphrase and visualize the given information and the steps as she solves problems. Carole wants to make sure Odessa begins to understand the details of a problem so she can think clearly about the relationships. Carole wants to provide her with as many real-life, authentic problem-solving opportunities as possible so that she can connect math to her world. Carole decides to have a volunteer tutor help Odessa set up and manage the class "pencil store" (see Chapter 2).

JOURNAL WRITING

A journal is a place where new ideas can be explored, where clarification and refinement takes place, or where a student can summarize, question, and react to his or her own work or to that of peers. Writing takes "talk" to that next level and should discuss the how, what, and why as students analyze and refine their thinking in a safe place. Many teachers use journals to have students answer questions, discover new ideas, or refine previously learned concepts. As we've described in earlier chapters, journals can be used for individual work before turn-and-talk, for recording questions for partner-reading, and for many other activities. Journal entries are also one of the most authentic, revealing pieces of assessment for the teacher.

Patti asked her second graders to write in their journals on the following: "Name your favorite shape. Draw a picture of a place where you would find it. Tell why it is your favorite." The students wrote responses to this during Writer's Workshop. At sharing time, as the students responded, they tallied the answers. This was a great resource for data collecting. Later the class created questions from the information on the chart. "What was the favorite shape of the whole class? What was the least favorite?" The next two writing experiences would be during math class using math journals. The first topic was planned to be a lead-in to the day's lesson. "Symmetry means . . . ." Students would also draw a picture. The next prompt would be at the end of the math unit: "Choose two shapes and discuss the similarities and differences on the Venn diagram. For example: cylinder/cone, pyramid/cone, or cube/rectangle prism." Patti found that this writing prompt really let her know who understood the concepts of select geometric shapes.

As described in Chapter 5, a Math Reading Strategies Bookmark (see Figure 5.3 can be used as a framework for writing in math journals. Sandy's fifth graders have a copy of the bookmark on the inside cover of their journals. It reminds them to read, think, paraphrase, visualize, represent, solve, explain, and justify. These fifth graders use their journals primarily for vocabulary development and problem-solving analysis. This record keeping of their thinking allows students to return to problems often, develop new understandings, and make connections to new material. ". . . the permanent quality of writing provides an important trail of children's thinking" (Whitin & Whitin, 2000, p. 17).

As we look at the students' journals, we can see the importance of guidelines like those in the Math Reading Strategies Bookmark. Because students are learning to read carefully and follow a sequence, their writing allows the teacher to see any misconceptions that students might have. Just as the solutions and explanations of math problems become more detailed over time, so do the recording of thoughts, solutions, strategies, and meaningful math vocabulary. Journals give teachers a way to look at an individual student's strategies for analyzing, clarifying, and refining his or her thinking. Not only can students explain their own work but they can react to other students' work (individually or as a group.) As with problem solving, younger students begin by drawing pictures to represent their understanding of a concept and their solution to a problem. Simple and/or detailed pictures gradually become symbolic representations rather than artistic drawings. Math pictures, symbols, and vocabulary become integrated as the student organizes and articulates his or her thoughts.

Since writing is a permanent artifact, it allows the teacher to analyze and reflect on the student's thoughts after the school day, unlike oral discussion, where reflection at a later time requires notetaking or audio taping. Many times the thinking that is revealed in math journals is not pleasant! Patti once gave a math writing prompt that stated, "Is 6–4 the same thing as 4–6?" To her dismay, two students thought they were the same. Needless to say, she planned reteaching time for those two students.

WRITING TO CLARIFY

The skill of writing requires one to think clearly. Students need to organize their thoughts by gathering information and then retelling that knowledge through writing. Initially, many students may not feel comfortable writing about math. However, through encouragement, modeling, and sharing classmates' thoughts, most students will eventually see the value of writing in math. If time is an issue, a teacher can occasionally provide opportunities for writing about math during Writer's Workshop. It need not take up the entire class time but may be part of a nonfiction writing segment.

One approach to helping students write with meaning is teaching them how to take notes and write in reaction to them. This is a skill that must be taught. It helps students retain what took place instructionally and then write to question and explore the mathematical ideas presented by either the teacher or class-mates.

After first modeling the note-taking skill for her third-grade class, Carole created simple booklets consisting of stapled sheets of paper. Students used these to take notes, copy problems, and/or react to the instruction being done at the board or on an overhead projector. This writing activity kept the students focused, observing and listening to the teacher and to each other. Students noted what they had heard by both sketching and writing. They were able to elaborate on their notes and list any questions or misconceptions that were not clear to them during the class discussion. Students learned that notetaking helps them organize and remember ideas that were generated by both the teacher and their peers. They also began to identify what might be important for future reference. One of Carole's students used his booklet to copy a problem and circle key words (e.g., *difference, high, low,* and *temperature*) before doing the mathematics. The student labeled the numbers in the problem as "high" and "low" and completed the subtraction problem, labeling his answer as the "difference." Other pages in his booklet showed attempts at clarifying place value and its importance in both addition and subtraction.

It is important for the teacher and students to know what concepts are understood and which ones are still confusing. Students in one fifth-grade class were asked to explain, in words, how they got an answer and why they took the particular steps to solving the given problem. The students write as they think through the meaning and the language of the problem and then the process of finding the solution. "I know that it had to be an even number and a multiple of 6 greater than 30 but less than 50." The rewording of the problem helps students think about what is really being asked and to estimate or predict possible answers before beginning the arithmetical work. "What do I know?" has helped students to organize their thinking as they begin to work on finding a solution. Do students see patterns and relationships sufficiently to explain them and give specific examples? Questions that ask children to think about the relationship between addition and multiplication, for example, are good indicators of a student's conceptual understanding. The booklets that Carole's students use have become an integral part of the math class.

WRITING PROMPTS

Writing prompts can ask students to respond to a specific question about a known process or mathematical content. These are called *content prompts*. A daily quick-write on a half sheet of paper or in a journal is a fast way to assess if the overall message of the lesson was achieved. *Attitude prompts* invite students to reflect about their attitude or feelings about themselves as mathematics students.

Content Prompts

Content prompts ask students to write about a previously taught concept chosen from the algebra, geometry, probability, measurement or number sense strands. The prompts might ask students for the following: to explain a mathematical symbol (e.g., what does = mean?); given a sequence of either numbers or shapes, to find and discuss the rule that created the pattern; to draw a picture that shows 3 + 5 = 5 + 3 and explain it; and to write about how a square and a rectangle are related? Because these prompts are chosen from what students already know, they are given the opportunity to use their prior knowledge. In one fifth-grade classroom, students were asked to respond to "Bridget says that decimals, fractions, and percents are all in a family. Why would she say that?" Students wrote about similarities, numerical value, written appearance, and relationships and gave specific examples of when each would be useful.

Attitude Prompts

Attitude prompts ask students to be introspective about their work as mathematicians. For example, they may be asked to articulate what they think a "good" math student does to solve a problem and/or relate it to their own work. At the end of the school year, Carole prompted her third-grade students to think about themselves when they were solving a math problem. Their writing was quite insightful.

One student was very direct: "A good math student shows their work and can explain it when they are solving a problem." Another student wrote about her own struggle: "I think that a good math student is when they don't shout out the answer. They let other people have a chance to think. That is a good math student." This student has become aware of her need for more time to think.

Responding to a writing prompt is purposeful and time should be carefully set aside for this work. As in all the work we do with writing, the teacher first models the activity during class instruction. The teacher's intentional selection of a particular prompt and establishing a dedicated time in which to respond gives importance to students' writing.

Teachers do not have to create their own prompts. There are books and materials available that provide good prompts such as those found in *The Write Way* by Barbara Dougherty. Carefully selected prompts will allow teacher and students and to see change and growth over time in students' attitudes and in their abilities to make connections within and between the mathematical concepts and the real world.

EXTENDED RESPONSE

As students are expected to write and communicate mathematically, teachers must model and discuss appropriate formats. One such format is called *extended response*. The student not only finds the answer or solution but explains how the solution was found and why. Typically, the extended response of each student is scored with a rubric that identifies several areas of math expertise. Most often, the student draws a picture or representation of how he or she thinks the problem can be solved, writes a number equation, and then provides a written explanation of the process used. We analyze their responses carefully to see which parts of the explaining and representing they do and do not understand. Ongoing assessment is essential as we craft scaffolds that lead students to the competencies described in the rubric. Many children are not comfortable with explaining their thoughts and just like to give the solution. We cannot stress enough the need for modeling and sharing responses of other students to support this type of writing.

CREATIVE WRITING AND STUDENT-WRITTEN PROBLEMS

To further motivate children and reinforce mathematical concepts we encourage students to create their own mathematical problems, poems, and stories. Younger students can work on stories and poems as a collaborative effort. Older students can be assigned creative writing with a specific purpose: defining a concept or mathematical operation and/or finding and using mathematics in their world. Writing a story allows students to show their understanding of both ordinary and mathematical vocabulary. The teacher can help keep students focused in their writing by giving them the key words to guide the story.

In early September, a third-grade student wrote this story: "My dog had 4 puppies. Then she had 2 more puppies. How many puppies did my dog have?" One month later, the same student wrote: "There are 90 children in the third grade going on a field trip to the zoo. In each bus there are 16 seats, three children to a seat. How many busses will they need to go on a field trip?" This student's writing has become more sophisticated in a short period of time and this continues as you look at later work. From these and other writings, the teacher can assess how the student has internalized particular concepts.

What a teacher sees and hears in class is not always an accurate assessment of the depth of student understanding. For example, after several days of teaching about multiplication and its complexities, students are asked to write their own multiplication number story. Some students' writing shows understanding of the concept but a few still write addition or subtraction stories. This assessment is helpful to the teacher in planning lessons.

Poetry

We want our students to enjoy the study of mathematics and to be active participants in their own learning. One way to do this is through the creative writing process. As discussed in Chapter 5, children who are actively engaged with literature can see mathematics connected to their daily lives and have a positive attitude about the study of mathematics.

Altieri (2005) suggests that formula poetry is an excellent way to use poetry in the mathematics classroom. "By connecting mathematical concepts with poetry, the teacher provides a positive, nurturing environment in which everyone can be successful and at the same time helps the children use their everyday experiences to reinforce mathematical concepts" (p. 18).

The type of formula poetry recommended does not require rhyme. Rather, repetition provides the framework. Students begin each line in a particular way or begin with a particular type of word. As we saw earlier, students in one second grade class used math words ending in -*ing* to write a poem. Patti's second-grade class created a poem using math words ending in -*tion*. Another poetry technique is the definition poem. Patti's class used this format to describe math as they knew it.

Math is . . .
   Dividing up whatever your favorite food is.
   Counting people in your class.
   An inch. An inch can measure a worm.
   Seeing what size your child is in pants and shirts.
   Measuring with a teaspoon.
   Dividing up the brownies your mom made with your brother.
   When you are looking at your clock to tell time.
   A pair of scissors.
   How far I can stretch.
   Multiplying how many pieces of pizza in three pizzas.
   Looking to see how much gas is.
   Shapes on a map.
   When you buy something.
   How many stripes a zebra has.

Each child in Patti's class contributed a line and then the class read the poem chorally. This poem was something the children and Patti came back to often—adding new ideas as their mathematical knowledge grew. These examples of definition and list poems provide ideas for reinforcing mathematical vocabulary.

Since most children enjoy poetry, including it in math class makes sense and offers further opportunities for writing and demonstrating their math knowledge. Students can also share their poetry with a larger audience such as another class or with parents at a literacy celebration. Altieri (2005) provides a number of activities and examples that teachers can use to generate poems based on math concepts. She also suggests using student-generated poems as assessments. The content of the poetry can provide a window into the students' understanding of concepts and vocabulary.

MATH PORTFOLIO

Collecting children's math writing over a period of time shows their thinking and what they know about mathematics. This is a wonderful tool to use during a parent conference or during a "Portfolio Night." There are many types of questions or prompts to include in a portfolio. Reflections on general math concepts may help plan instruction by using prompts such as "What is symmetry?" or "Explain how to use a counting number grid." Attitude prompts such as "What I like the best/least in math is _____," "I have trouble with _____," and "I learned something new about _____" are invitations for students to reflect on their own learning.

The portfolio may be a folder with math writing or a spiral notebook. Whatever organizational system the teacher chooses, the important thing is to include math writing within the unit. Whether used before, during, or after the unit, writing samples show student growth. Mathematical writing is an important tool; it builds confidence in our students, connects them to the real world, and provides insights into their mathematical understanding.

CHAPTER 8

MATH ASSESSMENT THROUGH LITERACY PRODUCTS

"My favorite math lesson is when we get to investigate . . . you're the teacher for yourself."—Karyn

"My favorite math lesson . . . I liked all the partner games. Because you could have a chance to kind of like help and teach each other."—Stacey

Reading these two student journal entries, Patti felt confident that a positive environment for mathematical thinking had been established in her classroom. Further, she saw that these students were engaged in pursuing their own learning. They were, on some level, monitoring what they knew and determining a line of inquiry that allowed them to learn more!

Teachers assess children either informally or formally every day on a variety of issues. These assessments guide the instruction in the classroom. In *Understanding by Design*, Wiggins and McTighe (1998, p. 7) describe teachers as "designers." "An essential act of our profession is the design of curriculum and learning experiences to meet specified purposes." Because of national, state, and local standards, teachers now have the job of making sure that all of our students meet the expectations set forth by these documents. Most of us are provided with a math curriculum that is based on standards and that informs how we proceed. State tests give information about how students are progressing in meeting the standards; weekly or unit tests show their achievement of smaller "chunks" of learning that lead to meeting the larger standards. But teachers must still design the day-to-day learning environment and the experiences that guide children toward these layers of achievement.

In an article in *American Educator*, Elmore (2005, p. 24) proposes that "[if] you walk into a classroom and sit down next to a student, ask him what he is doing and why, and you don't get a clear answer, it is highly unlikely that any powerful learning is taking place." For long-term learning to occur, students should be able to see the significance of what they are doing and how this meaning fits in a real-life situation. Planning for standards-based teaching "with the end in mind" has helped us to create this kind of environment for all students.

We now design instruction by first thinking specifically about what we want students to accomplish. State standards and assessments help define our priorities and influence choices we make in curriculum and pacing. Some tests assess problem-solving skills and communication skills of students. These tests do inform us and based on them, we adjust our understanding of what is important to emphasize in our teaching. We find out what the larger educational community thinks should be valued. Using the results of the state tests, we think about how our instruction may need to shift during the course of the year, for example, to include more problem solving, or to make more time for students to explain and justify their thinking. Think sheets and scaffolds like those used in previous chapters emerge from our observations of children as they work toward meeting the larger goals of the state test. Not only have the scaffolds provided support for our students, but they also represent benchmarks for our growth as teachers. Because we have needed to create these and other supports, we understand better how children come to be good at explaining their mathematical processes and problem-solving strategies.

By far the most abundant data we have about our students comes from the daily life of the classroom. Most of this data is conveyed in the form of literacy products: talking, writing, drawing, and responding to reading. Wiggins and McTighe (1998, p. 13) state, "Because understanding develops as a result of ongoing inquiry and rethinking, the assessment of understanding should be thought of in terms of a collection of evidence over time . . . " In math, these assessments include unit tests, quizzes, written and oral explanations, group interactions, journal writing, homework, teacher observations of students' problem-solving process, and more.

PREASSESSMENTS

In most schools, formal paper-and-pencil preassessments are given for different purposes at different points in the curriculum, but the pace of instruction is fast, and no one has time to formally preassess everything. Many preassessments are fairly quick and informal. Completing a KWL (What we Know, What we Want to Know, What we Learn) is exciting for students and provides a wealth of preassessment information for a teacher (see Chapter 3). Or, for a glimpse into students' background knowledge, what could be better than a vocabulary activity? For example, when Patti assesses second graders' knowledge of fractions she reads words such as *whole, halves, thirds,* and *fourths,* and the students shade the appropriate fractional part of a shape. At a glance Patti can tell generally how much her class remembers from the previous grade, and specifically which students are especially quick or which ones are confused. The next week, when the word study lesson includes these same fraction words, Patti provides the art activity called "fraction pies," in which students use fractional parts cut out of paper to make pies. Through this enjoyable activity, Patti can again observe which students are ready to apply the fraction concepts in the upcoming math unit.

Most of the literacy experiences described in this book may be used for preassessment: math talk; responding to reading; vocabulary building; writing about math, and so on. Observations of how students use manipulatives and tools such as rulers and calculators can also help teachers decide the course of instruction.

UNIT ASSESSMENTS

Assessments during and at the end of a unit of study provide snapshots of students' progress. Math writing and student math portfolios, discussed in Chapter 7, are two ways of assessing math units.

Just as important as the assessment itself is deciding how to proceed on the basis of the results. For example, on one unit assessment, Carole sees that two of her third graders do not know how to tell time as they are expected to. As she plans the next day's lesson, she knows that there will be some opportunities for students to tell time, so she plans to call on these two girls frequently. They happen to be seated next to each other that month so Carole plans to sit near them, ready to help, as they work on elapsed-time problems. She also plans for them to partner-read a book about telling time at a learning center during reading class that week. A colleague suggests the following teaching strategy for teaching children to tell time:

> "I have my children come up to my desk for a little reward sticker. I give each child a little card with a time written on it. During the day, when it is the time on the card, the child who has it quietly hands me the card (or places it down by me). I then give the child the sticker or stamp as a reward. For differentiation, some students might have just the time written on the card, whereas others may have an elapsed time, such as '20 minutes later than 10:15.' "

On the same unit assessment, Alphonse completes almost none of the items correctly. Carole consults with the learning resource teacher who also works with him, and they decide that the resource teacher will go over the test with him the next day. After doing so, the resource teacher sends Carole a note: "Alphonse does not understand area and perimeter." That afternoon Carole is planning to introduce a "Concept Definition Map" to the class (see Chapter 6) and decides to use the terms *area* and *perimeter* as examples for a class think-aloud. During the class discussion, she is able to call on Alphonse to elicit and use his words on the class's think sheet defining *area* as *the inside of a shape*.

It is not always easy to use the data from unit tests to make decisions about instruction. Trying to keep track of many students' needs and to devise specialized lessons to address all of them while moving ahead in the curriculum, can quickly become overwhelming. But even choosing a few specific issues to address with one or two children, as Carole did in the examples above, can be worthwhile. To make those choices, we refer to priorities defined by local and state standards.

INTERVIEWS AND MATH INVENTORIES

Occasionally, it is beneficial to interview students about what they think of math and how they are learning. This process shows students that the teacher respects their thoughts and opinions. The opportunity to self-assess sends a message to students that they have some responsibility in the learning process. It also may send the message that children can make choices that will influence how well they learn. Depending on what information the teacher is interested in finding out, some questions may be:

"How do you feel about math?"
"What has been the easiest and the hardest part of math?"
"What strategies help you when you get stuck?"
"How do you feel about small-group activities?"

Math inventories also assess students' attitudes about math and the math classroom environment. Inventories may be easily included a few times a year as part of the unit tests. They are much like the interviews described above, but in a simple paper-and-pencil format where responses can be easily marked. The document can then be added to enhance a student's portfolio and discussed individually or at the parent conference. It is very interesting to notice if students' attitudes change throughout the year.

PARENT INVOLVEMENT

Periodically, the parents may be included in the assessment. Sending an information sheet home about math before or after a parent conference may promote a thoughtful conference that encourages parents' help and support. Another tool is a conference response sheet that children and parents complete together during the conference. An example of the one Carole uses for third grade is seen in Figure 8.1. With guidance from the teacher, students and parents work together to review student work and to set goals.

Carole prepares children in advance so they know what will be expected as they complete the sheet with their parents. Sometimes there is not enough time for them to complete it during the conference under the teacher's watchful eye. When this is the case, Carole takes a few moments to make sure the parent knows what to do, and then sends the sheet with them to be filled out at home. The child then returns the completed form to school the next day. On the Student and Parent Conference Sheet, the parent first writes a compliment about a specific piece of their child's work. Carole asks for this first to make sure that parents take time to appreciate the positive aspects of the child's work before becoming critical. It is reassuring to many students to know in advance that this will set the tone for the discussion. This also gives the teacher a chance to "coach" the parent, pointing out to them some important successes shown by the work that they might want to mention in their comments. Next, parent and student confer to determine what improvement they would both like to see. Carole gently coaches families through this interaction.

Assessments discussed in this section are done somewhat formally at the end of a unit or extended period of time, such as a trimester. In the following section we focus on assessments we make daily in the course of classroom life.

ASSESSING AND ADJUSTING DAILY WORK IN THE CLASSROOM

Assessments made through observation of children and their work in the classroom are essential to the decisions we make from moment to moment as we adjust instruction to meet students' needs. The better a teacher gets at making astute observations and at using them to make purposeful, informed decisions about instruction as a lesson unfolds, the more students will be individually challenged, engaged, and actively learning. The aim is to maximize the learning for every child at every moment. For this reason we include here a separate section devoted to assessment that is done in every lesson and that informs instruction in the classroom immediately as well as for the long term.

We observe, for example, a student's computation process as she works on a subtraction problem and see where she has misconceptions about the place value system. While we can use a test or worksheet to verify our observations and to take time for carefully analyzing the work, many of the best insights we have about stu-

Name _____

STUDENT AND PARENT CONFERENCE
Winter

Math: Extended Responses

Parent Compliment: _____

_____

_____

What we would like to improve: _____

_____

Reading: Extended Responses

Parent Compliment: _____

_____

_____

What we would like to improve: _____

_____

Inquiry Research: Reading/Notetaking/Organizing

Parent Compliment: _____

_____

_____

What we would like to improve: _____

_____

FIGURE 8.1. Student and parent conference sheet.

dents' thinking come from their talking, writing, and responses to reading in the classroom.

As students talk about math and play math games, are they challenged? Is a given lesson too easy or obvious for most of the children? Can we speed up our delivery and meet the needs of all of our students? Is the lack of background knowledge of a few students regulating the pace of the curriculum? How can we make adjustments? For these questions, the teacher is in the unique and all-important position of knowing the best answers for his or her classroom.

The following are some general tips for adjusting instruction for the whole class on the basis of daily assessments.

Giving Students Enough Think Time

How do you challenge all students with one problem? In any group there are students who usually find the solution quickly, followed by other students who will find the solution in a reasonable amount of time, followed by students who are not confident with any strategies to solve problems.

Patti gave her second graders the following problem:

Sue wanted to make a bead bracelet for her sister. First she put a yellow bead on the string. Next, she put a pink bead on the string. Last, she put a green bead on the string. She decided to continue the pattern. What color will the ninth bead be?

As students worked on the problem, Patti walked around the room observing. She has found that most children will be invested in finding the solution if she quietly encourages them. Simple comments such as "good idea," "you can do it," or "nice try" can go a long way to involve all students in the thinking process. For the few students who found the solution quickly—their hands raised, bursting to tell the answer—Patti reminded them that this is "think time" and to make sure they could explain how they got the answer or what strategy they used. As these students reviewed their work to see if they had included explanations and strategies, other students found the solution. Patti waited until she sensed that most of the class had found a solution. Rather than first asking for answers, she supported the few who were not yet successful by asking the class for a strategy they used. One child reported that he drew a picture to help him find the answer. Patti suggested that students could try this strategy if they needed help finding a solution. After a short time, the class shared their answers and explained their strategies. Quinn explained, "I did not draw a picture but wrote the color words until I got to the ninth word." Lesley said, "I just used my fingers and said the colors to repeat the pattern." Gillian had written the number sentence 3 + 3 + 3 = 9 and said, "I wrote above the number sentence the words *yellow, pink, green* and drew an arrow to each addend."

This activity took a short amount of time but was filled with teacher assessments and strategic decisions, such as how much "think time" was needed to get as many students as possible to participate. When Patti saw the relative ease with which most children figured out this pattern she decided that her class was ready to advance quickly into more complex problem solving.

Choosing a Problem the Whole Class Can Work On

Carole wanted the whole class to be engaged as they worked through a problem. This meant the problem needed to challenge the most capable math students while being accessible to everyone. She did not want the "fast thinkers" to solve it with little effort and then become disinterested while she supported others still working through it. She decided to look at math problems the children had themselves written to remind herself about their problem-solving strengths and weaknesses.

One problem stood out. Stephen and Peter had collaborated to write:

> George was reading a book that was 900 pages. On the first day he read 250 pages. On the second day he read double the amount he read on the first day. How many pages does he have left to read?

When Stephen and Peter solved their problem they doubled 250, getting 500. Then they subtracted 500 from 900 and concluded that George had 400 pages left to read. Only after working on the solution for some time and receiving big hints from the teacher, did they realize that they had neglected to subtract the 250 pages read on the first day. This indicated to Carole that the boys were familiar with the wording of a two-step problem, but did not quite understand how to go about solving it. They had shown the cognitive "edge" of their understanding. Keeping this in mind, Carole selected a two-part problem that could be solved with a "guess-and-check" procedure.

Adjusting the Delivery Method or Pacing of a Lesson

As every good teacher knows, not everything can be planned in advance. But a good teacher is aware of options, or ways to respond, depending on what happens in class. Pacing is important. When do we slow down; when do we speed up? In one lesson, Patti's second-grade class collected data by using tally marks to show the number of children who chose a favorite food in each food group. Then the children made a graph of this data. Patti circulated, observed, and listened to conversations. What she saw and heard told her that the children seemed to understand the concept of that day's lesson. Not one student needed assistance with the use of tally marks or how to read a graph. She reminded them to be aware of the numbers along the side of the graph and to be careful of how far up to draw each bar. The groundwork had been laid. Because the children had been exposed to graphs frequently through social studies topics and through class discussions, it made sense that this lesson was a breeze.

So Patti made a pacing decision. She decided not to spend much time discussing the graph and moved to the next part of the lesson.

Another example follows from Carole's introduction of area to her third graders as described in Chapter 6. Following the definition of the term, the children worked with partners to find the area of the classroom floor using square-yard papers. Carole circulated, observing and listening in on conversations. Most students were putting papers around the edges of the room. Someone said, "We found out how far it is from here to that wall. It is 2 yards." Another student said, "You could just make one row and then count the rows." Another student asked Carole if they were finding area or perimeter. Carole reminded her that they were trying to find out how many squares it would take to cover the whole floor. Steven and Peter, discussing the problem, said that, "perimeter can help you find the area because you can find out one row and then multiply it by the number of rows."

Carole realized that Steven and Peter had articulated something that she observed most of the children doing. No one appeared to be trying to cover the whole floor with squares—they were figuring out that they could make one row along the edge and somehow go from there. Carole determined that they were all pretty close to getting the concept of multiplying length times width to find the area. The students certainly understood the concept of area as the number of smaller squares needed to cover up the inside of the larger shape. Based on this assessment, Carole made a pacing decision; because the groundwork had been laid, she could more quickly through the rest of the lesson—the part where she shows them how to find area by counting the squares inside a shape.

Reflecting on their experiences in the previous days, Carole decided that the students were well on their way to being ready for the next day's lesson—finding area by multiplying length times width. And, given their current understanding, Carole decided to address the expression, *by*—as in a "5 *by* 7 rectangle"—that appeared on an activity sheet they had worked on earlier that day.

As the above sequence of lessons makes clear, Carole assessed the students' use of language and their ability to articulate their understanding of the process. This assessment led to her decisions about the amount of scaffolding needed, the kinds of experiences needed next, and when to introduce the correct terminology. The ongoing assessment also provided information necessary for making decisions about pacing and for deciding who needed additional support.

Assessing One Child and Making an Instructional Decision for the Whole Class

Carole asked her third-grade class to retell and draw a diagram for the following problem:

> Michae has 50 pencils. Some are fancy pencils and some are plain pencils. She has 14 fewer fancy pencils than plain pencils. How many pencils of each kind does she have?

Carole wondered if this was going to be an appropriate exercise for Peter. She thought he might be able to understand the problem quickly because he had recently worked on paraphrasing and visualizing a similar problem. Near the end of the writing session, Peter got Carole's attention. He was excited to tell her about his discovery.

> "Look, Mrs. Skalinder, I knew that there are 14 fewer fancy pencils. So I tried 30. Thirty plain pencils. I subtracted 14 to find out how many fancy pencils. That was 16. But look . . . the total of all the pencils has to be 50. 16 plus 30 is only 46. I need more. So then I tried 32. 32 – 14 equals 18. 18 plus 32 is 50!"

Carole recognized that, while the rest of the class was working on the retelling, Peter had discovered a guess-and-check method for solving the problem. She now knew that this was a good task for him. It gave him the opportunity to work at his cognitive "edge." Peter had been challenged and was successful! Secondly, she recognized that they now had a new opportunity. The next time the class encounters a problem that invites a guess-and-check solution process, Carole will ask Peter to articulate and explain his process. This will be a chance for him to reinforce his understanding and to provide leadership for the class's thinking.

Assessing Understanding through Math Games and Talk

When students are playing math games, the teacher has opportunities for assessing, not only social skills and general behavior, but also students' understanding of math concepts and instructions. When our students struggle with math, our observations in the daily life of the classroom are especially critical. For example, how a student uses manipulatives can help teachers understand a child's thinking and so decide appropriate supports.

We keep observation notes on a clipboard or put a few comments along with the date on an index card. So many times we intend to write our thoughts down, but with the sheer pace of the day, we get sidetracked and often forget the details. But we need this information. It can help us meet students' individual needs. When there is an opportunity for small-group instruction or conferencing the teacher can rely upon this data. It is a perfect time to assess what students know when they are having math discussions in small groups or playing games.

Many of us have played Pin the Tail on the Donkey when we were young. A similar game using the hundred chart provides information about a child's number sense. A child is given a sticky note and closes his or her eyes. He or she stands fairly close to the hundred chart and the teacher says a number such as 42. The child tries to guess where 42 is without looking and places the sticky note on the chart. Everyone enjoys seeing how close the child came to knowing where the number was on the chart. Patti played the game with her students one day. A girl who had some difficulty with math concepts wanted to play. Patti said the number 75. The child had no idea in what general direction to look for the number 75. Actually, a game format is not even necessary to assess number sense using the hundred chart. Teachers can just ask a student to point to a number and see if they have a general sense of where that number is located in relationship to other numbers.

Homework

Homework provides additional information that teachers use to make adjustments to instruction. In some math programs, the lead question of the lesson involves concepts used in the previous day's homework. In this way, students are exposed to the concept again without necessarily going over the homework sheet. We encourage students to let us know when they have not understood the homework. Students know that we will then spend a few minutes going over it.

When Patti reviewed one second-grade homework assignment about giving change, half of the students either misunderstood the directions or had difficulty in this area. She then knew to provide additional experiences with money and giving change.

A CASE STUDY OF ASSESSMENT AND TAILORED INSTRUCTION

Daniel came to our third-grade class from another school. The report that came with him said that he was making progress in reading, but was still working more than a year below grade level in math. When Carole introduced the word *difference*, the class talked about the "ordinary" meaning of the word. Two children are not identical; they have various "differences." For a definition of the word, Daniel wrote, "Some books are difference." When prompted to use the word in a sentence, he wrote, "Mrs. Skalinder is nice." Five weeks later, when the class was given another think sheet for the same word, Daniel drew a picture of two boys with very different hair, and wrote the sentence, "Two boys are different." Seeing this, Carole noted that some progress was taking place. This language-based assessment gave Carole information about how to move Daniel forward.

The next day she arranged a conference with Daniel and another child as they worked on subtraction problems. She reminded Daniel about the two boys on his vocabulary paper:

TEACHER: Are they exactly alike, or are they different?

DANIEL: They are different.

TEACHER: Are these two numbers (18, 34) the same?

DANIEL: No, they are different. This one is more.

TEACHER: How much more? Let's see here, on this number grid.

Together they practiced counting up on the number grid from 18 to 34 to find the difference.

In this particular case, the process of alternating assessment and instruction was successful. The next day Daniel became an active participant in the math class when Carole asked him to show his strategy to the class.

"So, Daniel has shown us a way to find the difference by counting up. We will call this method 'Daniel's method.' "

She wrote a summary of Daniel's method on a class chart and labeled it "Daniel's method."

On another day soon after, Carole taught a lesson in which children wrote their own problems involving multidigit addition and subtraction. She gave the children several examples. Keeping in mind Daniel's successes with the "counting up" strategy, Carole offered the following example:

The Gold team has 18 points. The Purple team has 27 points. How many points does the Gold team need in order to catch up?

Most children wrote their own problem after reading the example. However, Carole knew that for Daniel to be successful, he would need to choose one of the given models and solve it. He not only did that successfully, but significantly, he chose the one problem the teacher had constructed specifically to illustrate an application of his "counting up" method.

Carole continued to praise Daniel's problem solving at every possible opportunity. Although he worked at a level below his peers, Daniel maintained enthusiasm for math and problem solving throughout the year. He progressed at a faster rate than he had in previous grades.

In the spring, when looking at a broad range of test scores for Daniel, the school support team noticed a surprising result. In Mathematics Problem Solving, Daniel scored significantly above the level predicted from his other scores. It seems to us that sensitive use of language-based classroom assessments and subsequent adjusting of instruction for this child contributed significantly to this success.

Teachers need to be mindful of the timetable of high-stakes testing. If they are confident in their math program and provide opportunities for math talk and writing, their students will be successful. More importantly, they will be lifelong learners of math!

CONCLUSION

The authors know that teachers do the kinds of assessment described here all the time. Our observations as staff developers and our years of interactions with colleagues confirm this. It is what we do. Assessments inform our instruction constantly. We observe and listen to students; we make multiple decisions every minute about how to respond to them and how to proceed with the lessons we teach. We look closely at the thinking revealed in children's writing and talking about mathematics and we respond to that thinking directly in our instruction. In doing so, we know that we are working with our students at their zone of proximal development. Armed with this information, we create lessons and provide the necessary scaffolds so students experience success in our math classes. We want more students to feel like Ahmed, who quietly exclaimed to his teacher after the math lesson, "That made our minds work and it was fun!"

NCTM STANDARDS FOR SCHOOL MATHEMATICS

NUMBER AND OPERATIONS STANDARD

Instructional programs from prekindergarten through grade 12 should enable all students to:

➢ Understand numbers, ways of representing numbers, relationships among numbers, and number systems;

➢ Understand meanings of operations and how they relate to one another;

➢ Compute fluently and make reasonable estimates.

ALGEBRA STANDARD

Instructional programs from prekindergarten through grade 12 should enable all students to:

➢ Understand patterns, relations, and functions;

➢ Represent and analyze mathematical situations and structures using algebraic symbols;

➢ Use mathematical models to represent and understand quantitative relationships;

➢ Analyze change in various contexts.

GEOMETRY STANDARD

Instructional programs from prekindergarten through grade 12 should enable all students to:

> ➢ Analyze characteristics and properties of two- and three-dimensional geometric shapes and develop mathematical arguments about geometric relationships;
> ➢ Specify locations and describe spatial relationships using coordinate geometry and other representational systems;
> ➢ Apply transformations and use symmetry to analyze mathematical situations;
> ➢ Use visualization, spatial reasoning, and geometric modeling to solve problems.

MEASUREMENT STANDARD

Instructional programs from prekindergarten through grade 12 should enable all students to:

> ➢ Understand measurable attributes of objects and the units, systems, and processes of measurement;
> ➢ Apply appropriate techniques, tools, and formulas to determine measurements.

DATA ANALYSIS AND PROBABILITY STANDARD

Instructional programs from prekindergarten through grade 12 should enable all students to:

> ➢ Formulate questions that can be addressed with data and collect, organize, and display relevant data to answer them;
> ➢ Select and use appropriate statistical methods to analyze data;
> ➢ Develop and evaluate inferences and predictions that are based on data;
> ➢ Understand and apply basic concepts of probability.

PROBLEM-SOLVING STANDARD

Instructional programs from prekindergarten through grade 12 should enable all students to:

> ➢ Build new mathematical knowledge through problem solving;
> ➢ Solve problems that arise in mathematics and in other contexts;
> ➢ Apply and adapt a variety of appropriate strategies to solve problems;
> ➢ Monitor and reflect on the process of mathematical problem solving.

REASONING AND PROOF STANDARD

Instructional programs from prekindergarten through grade 12 should enable all students to:

➢ Recognize reasoning and proof as fundamental aspects of mathematics;
➢ Make and investigate mathematical conjectures;
➢ Develop and evaluate mathematical arguments and proofs;
➢ Select and use various types of reasoning and methods of proof.

COMMUNICATION STANDARD

Instructional programs from prekindergarten through grade 12 should enable all students to:

➢ Organize and consolidate their mathematical thinking through communication;
➢ Communicate their mathematical thinking coherently and clearly to peers, teachers, and others;
➢ Analyze and evaluate the mathematical thinking and strategies of others;
➢ Use the language of mathematics to express mathematical ideas precisely.

CONNECTIONS STANDARD

Instructional programs from prekindergarten through grade 12 should enable all students to:

➢ Recognize and use connections among mathematical ideas;
➢ Understand how mathematical ideas interconnect and build on one another to produce a coherent whole;
➢ Recognize and apply mathematics in contexts outside of mathematics.

REPRESENTATION STANDARD

Instructional programs from prekindergarten through grade 12 should enable all students to:

➢ Create and use representations to organize, record, and communicate mathematical ideas;
➢ Select, apply, and translate among mathematical representations to solve problems;
➢ Use representations to model and interpret physical, social, and mathematical phenomena.

STANDARDS FOR THE ENGLISH LANGUAGE ARTS OF THE NCTE AND THE IRA

The vision guiding these standards is that all students must have the opportunities and resources to develop the language skills they need to pursue life's goals and to participate fully as informed, productive members of society. These standards assume that literacy growth begins before children enter school as they experience and experiment with literacy activities—reading, and writing, and associating spoken words with their graphic representations. Recognizing this fact, these standards encourage the development of curriculum and instruction that make productive use of the emerging literary abilities that children bring to school. Furthermore, the standards provide ample room for the innovation and creativity essential to teaching and learning. They are not prescriptions for particular curriculum or instruction.

Although we present these standards as a list, we want to emphasize that they are not distinct and separable; they are, in fact, interrelated and should be considered as a whole.

1. Students read a wide range of print and nonprint texts to build on understanding of texts, of themselves, and of the cultures of the United States and the world; to acquire new information; to respond to the needs and demands of society and the workplace; and for personal fulfillment. Among these texts are fiction and nonfiction, classic and contemporary works.

2. Students read a wide range of literature from many periods in many genres to build an understanding of the many dimensions (e.g., philosophical, ethical, aesthetic) of human experience.

---

3. Students apply a wide range of strategies to comprehend, interpret, evaluate, and appreciate texts. They draw on their prior experience, their interactions with other readers and writers, their knowledge of word meaning and of other texts, their word identification strategies, and their understanding of textual features (e.g., sound–letter correspondence, sentence structure, context, graphics).

4. Students adjust their use of spoken, written, and visual language (e.g., conventions, style, vocabulary) to communicate effectively with a variety of audiences and for different purposes.

5. Students employ a wide range of strategies as they write and use different writing process elements appropriately to communicate with different audiences for a variety of purposes.

6. Students apply knowledge of language structure, language conventions (e.g., spelling and punctuation), media techniques, figurative language, and genre to create, critique, and discuss print and nonprint texts.

7. Students conduct research on issues and interests by generating ideas and questions, and by posing problems. They gather, evaluate, and synthesize data from a variety of sources (e.g., print and nonprint texts, artifacts, people) to communicate their discoveries in ways that suit their purpose and audience.

8. Students use a variety of technological and information resources (e.g., libraries, databases, computer networks, video) to gather and synthesize information and to create and communicate knowledge.

9. Students develop an understanding of and respect for diversity of language use, patterns, and dialects across cultures, ethnic groups, geographic regions, and social roles.

10. Students whose first language is not English make use of their first language to develop competency in the English language arts and to develop understanding of content across the curriculum.

11. Students participate as knowledgeable, reflective, creative, and critical members of a variety of literacy communities.

12. Students use spoken, written, and visual language to accomplish their own purposes (e.g., for learning, enjoyment, persuasion, and the exchange of information).

TEACHERS' FAVORITE READ-ALOUDS

A Cloak for the Dreamer by Aileen Friedman (Scholastic)

How geometric shapes fit together is one of the underlying questions in this beautifully illustrated story. The story is about a tailor and his three sons and how they design their cloaks. In addition to the real-world application, the story has a lovely message about following your own dream. Usually the children create patterns using more than one shape after the reading, using templates or pattern blocks.

A Million Fish . . . More or Less by Patricia C. McKissack (Knopf)

This is one of the all-time favorite third-grade read-alouds among all genres, not just among math-related books. It takes place in the "Bayou Clapateaux," where the exaggerated fishing claims of Hugh Thomas increase quantitatively as he encounters a series of tricky characters, including a raccoon named Mosley and a beguiling cat named Chantilly.

One year Carole Skalinder's class wrote stories inspired by this book. First they wrote narratives about an ordinary event. Then they rewrote the stories, using huge numbers as one of the devices to create wild exaggeration.

Even Steven and Odd Todd by Kathryn Cristaldi (Scholastic)

Almost every year this book is voted Book of the Week in the second-grade classroom. The story is very clever and is a wonderful review of the concepts of even and odd numbers. By the end of the story the children are giggling at how Even Steven reacts to his cousin's odd ways! There are many activity suggestions at the end of the book.

Grandfather Tang's Story by Ann Tompert (Crown)

This is the perfect book to lead into a discussion about tangrams. The story is so compelling that some of the students fear for the animal characters. After the read-aloud, have the children try to make animals using a set of tangrams. Then they can write their own tale about their animal.

Grapes of Math by Greg Tang (Scholastic)

This is a great book for fifth-grade students because the problems are fun and it inspires good discussion about different ways to solve a problem. In it, students look at patterns as groupings or shapes to figure out the number of objects without counting them. Even though this book is used as a read-aloud, it is one that is often picked from the bookshelf and studied by individuals as many students are interested in finding other ways to solve the problems presented.

The Greedy Triangle by Marilyn Burns (Scholastic)

This creative story about two-dimensional shapes is very appealing to children. The shapes come alive with colorful illustrations. The wonderful list of places to find these shapes in the world leads the children to find the geometric shapes in the classroom.

The Greenwich Guide to Measuring Time by Graham Dolan (Heinemann)

This book from the Royal Observatory in Greenwich, Great Britain, describes the history of telling time. Many students are surprised to learn that clocks are not just a given natural phenomenon. They are tools that have been invented and gradually improved to measure more and more accurately the passing of time as it is observed in our universe.

Is a Blue Whale the Biggest Thing There Is? by Robert E. Wells (Whitman)

When third graders start to work with numbers that are "ten times as much as" or "a hundred times as much as" other numbers, they need help visualizing the magnitude of such quantities. They are fascinated by this book because it provides just what they need!

The Librarian Who Measured the Earth by Kathryn Lasky (Little, Brown)

This is a good book to use during a geometry unit. It is great for a multidisciplinary lesson as it is a combination of history, math, and geography. It is a picture book, in a biographical format, of Erothosthanes and how he calculated the size of the Earth.

One Grain of Rice by Demi (Scholastic)

This mathematical folktale is beautifully illustrated with foldout pages to show the number of rice grains accumulated at various points in the story. The children's eyes usually widen in awe when they see these pages. It is a story for all grade levels. A chart at the end of the book explains how one grain of rice grows to over one billion grains. There are many opportunities for place value lessons in this story!

One Hundred Hungry Ants by Elinor J. Pinczes (Scholastic)

This cute book is written in rhyme and shows different arrays for one hundred. It should be read more than once. On the second reading, use manipulatives and have the children form the different arrays. *A Remainder of One* by Elinor J. Pinczes is also a clever book to use with manipulatives.

Pigs Will Be Pigs by Amy Axelrod (Four Winds Press)

Third-grade students find this book hilarious. It provides many opportunities for adding and subtracting various amounts of money as the pigs run all over their house looking for enough small change to eat out at a restaurant. After reading the book, the students calculate the cost of various possible selections from the enticing menu at the end.

Sir Cumference and the First Round Table: A Math Adventure by Cindy Neuschwander (Charlesbridge)

This is a clever book that explains circumference, diameter, and radius. The story is engaging and the characters are appealing. It is a good way to help fifth-grade students remember and understand circle concepts.

Other resources for read-alouds include *Wonderful World of Mathematics* (Thiessen, Mathias, & Smith, 1998), *Read Any Good Math Lately?* (Wilde & Whitin, 1992), and *Books You Can Count On: Linking Mathematics and Literature* (Griffiths & Clyne, 1991).

REFERENCES

Adams, T. (2003). Reading mathematics: More than words can say. *The Reading Teacher,* 56(8), 786–795.

Allington, R., & Johnston, P. (2002). Integrated instruction in exemplary fourth-grade classrooms. In *Reading to learn: Lessons from exemplary fourth-grade classrooms* (pp. 169–187). New York: Guilford Press.

Altieri, J. (2005). Creating poetry: Reinforcing mathematical concepts. *Teaching Children Mathematics, 12*(1), 18–23.

Association of Teachers of Mathematics in Maine. (2000, Winter). I have, who has? *Association of Teachers of Mathematics in Maine Newsletter,* p. 11.

Ball, D. L., & Bass, H. (2001). What mathematical knowledge is entailed in teaching children to reason mathematically? In National Research Council, *Knowing and learning mathematics for teaching* (pp. 26–34). Washington, DC: National Academy Press.

Bamford, R., & Kristo, J. (1998). *Making facts come alive: Choosing quality nonfiction literature K–8.* Norwood, MA: Christopher-Gordon.

Barton, M., Heidema, C., & Jordan, D. (2002). Teaching reading in mathematics and science. *Educational Leadership, 50*(3), 24–28.

Bear, D., Invernizzi, M., Templeton, S., & Johnston, F. (2007). *Words their way* (4th ed.). Parsippany, NJ: Pearson Learning Group.

Beck, I., McKeown, M., Hamilton, R., & Kucan, L. (1997). *Questioning the author.* Newark, DE: International Reading Association.

Beck, I., McKeown, M., & Kucan, L. (2002). *Bringing words to life.* New York: Guilford Press.

Bell, M., Bell, J., Bretzlauf, J., Dillard, A., Hartfield, R., Isaacs, A., et al. (2001). *Everyday mathematics student reference book (grade 3).* Chicago: Everyday Learning.

Bell, M., Bell, J., Bretzlauf, J., Dillard, A., Hartfield, R., Isaacs, A., et al. (2002a). *Everyday mathematics student reference book (grade 4).* Chicago: Everyday Learning.

Bell, M., Bell, J., Bretzlauf, J., Dillard, A., Hartfield, R., Isaacs, A., et al. (2004b). *Everyday mathematics student reference book (grade 5).* Chicago: SRA/McGraw-Hill.

Berlin, D. (2003). Integrated mathematics: From models to practice. In S. McGraw (Ed.), *Integrated mathematics: Choices and challenges* (pp. 43–57). Reston, VA: National Council of Teachers of Mathematics.

Blachowicz, C., & Fisher, P. (2002). *Teaching vocabulary in all classrooms* (2nd ed.). Englewood Cliffs, NJ: Merrill/Prentice-Hall.

Blachowicz, C., Fisher, P., Ogle, D., & Watts-Taffe, S. (2006). Vocabulary: Questions from the classroom. *Reading Research Quarterly, 41*(4), 524–539.

Blachowicz, C., & Ogle, D. (2001). *Reading comprehension strategies for independent learners.* New York: Guilford Press.

Bresser, R. (1995). *Math and literature grades 4–6.* Sausalito, CA: Math Solutions.

Brown, H., & Cambourne, B. (1990). *Read and retell.* Portsmouth, NH: Heinemann.

Chicago Board of Education. (2006). *Nonfiction leveled text sets: Social studies teachers guide.* Chicago: Chicago Public School Literacy.

Daniels, H. (2002). *Literature circles: Voice and choice in book clubs and reading groups.* Portland, ME: Stenhouse.

Daniels, H., & Zemelman, S. (2004). *Subjects matter: Every teacher's guide to content-area reading.* Portsmouth, NH: Heinemann.

Davey, B. (1983). Think aloud: Modeling the cognitive processes of reading comprehension. *Journal of Reading, 27*(1), 44–47.

Dorn, L. J., & Soffos, C. (2001). *Shaping literate minds.* Portland, ME: Stenhouse.

Dougherty, B. J. (2002). *The "write way": Mathematics journal prompts for grades 3–4.* Honolulu: University of Hawaii Curriculum Research and Development Group.

Draper, R. J. (2002). School mathematics reform, constructivism, and literacy. *Journal of Adult and Adolescent Literacy, 45*(6), 520–529.

Duke, N., & Bennett-Armistead, S. (2003). *Reading and writing informational text in the primary grades.* New York: Scholastic.

Elmore, R. (2005). Building new knowledge: School improvement requires new knowledge, not just good will. *American Educator, 29*(1), 20–27.

Frayer, D. A., Frederick, W. C., & Klausmeier, H. G. (1969). A schema for testing the level of concept mastery. *Working paper No. 16.* Madison: University of Wisconsin.

Graves, M. (2006). *The vocabulary book: Learning and instruction.* New York: Teachers College Press.

Griffiths, R., & Clyne, M. (1991). *Books you can count on: Linking mathematics and literature.* Portsmouth, NH: Heinemann.

Harvey, S. (1998). *Nonfiction matters: Reading, writing, and research in grades 3–8.* York, ME: Stenhouse.

Harvey, S., & Goudvis, A. (2000). *Strategies that work: Teaching comprehension for understanding and engagement.* York, ME: Stenhouse.

Harvey, S., & Goudvis, A. (2007). *Strategies that work* (2nd ed.). Portland, ME: Stenhouse.

Heuer, L. (2005). Graphic representation in the mathematics classroom. In J. M. Kenney, E. Hancewicz, L. Heuer, D. Metsisto, & C. Tuttle (Eds.), *Literacy strategies for improving mathematics instruction* (pp. 51–71). Alexandria, VA: Association for Supervision and Curriculum Development.

Hoogeboom, S., & Goodnow, J. (1987). *The problem solver 2.* Sunnyvale, CA: Creative.

House, P. (2003). Integrated mathematics: An introduction. In S. McGraw (Ed.), *Integrated mathematics: Choices and challenges* (pp. 3–11). Reston, VA: National Council of Teachers of Mathematics.

Howden, H. (1990). Prior experiences. In E. Edwards, Jr. (Ed.), *Algebra for everyone* (pp. 7–23). Reston, VA: National Council of Teachers of Mathematics.

Hoyt, L. (1999). *Revisit, reflect, retell: Strategies for improving reading comprehension.* Portsmouth, NH: Heinemann.

Hoyt, L., Mooney, M., & Parkes, B. (2003). *Exploring informational texts.* Portsmouth, NH: Heinemann.

Hufferd-Ackles, K., Fuson, K., & Sherin, M. (2004). Describing levels and components of a math-talk learning community. *Journal for Research in Mathematics Education, 35,* 81–116.

Hunsader, P. (2004). Mathematics trade books: Establishing their value and assessing their quality. *The Reading Teacher, 57*(7), 618–629.

Hyde, A. (2006). *Comprehending math: Adapting reading strategies to teach mathematics, K–6.* Portsmouth, NH: Heinemann.

Jiminez, R. J. (1997). The strategic reading abilities and potential of five low-literacy Latina/o readers in middle school. *Reading Research Quarterly, 32,* 224–243.

Johnston, P. (2004). *Choice words.* Portland, ME: Stenhouse.

Kenney, J. (2005). Mathematics as language. In J. Kenney, E. Hancewicz, L. Heuer, D. Metsisto, & C. Tuttle (Eds.), *Literacy strategies for improving mathematics instruction* (pp. 1–8). Alexandria, VA: Association for Supervision and Curriculum Development.

Kump, L. (2001). *Math: Using cognitive strategies in math.* Available at readinglady.com.

Laminack, L., & Wadsworth, R. (2006). *Learning under the influence of language and literature.* Portsmouth, NH: Heinemann.

Leitze, A. (1997). Connecting process problem solving to children's literature. *Teaching Children Mathematics, 3*(7), 398–406.

Lott, J., & Reeves, C. (1991, April). The integrated mathematics project. *Mathematics Teacher, 84,* 334–335.

Marzano, R. (2004). *Building background knowledge for academic achievement.* Alexandria, VA: Association for Supervision and Curriculum Development.

Marzano, R., Pickering, D., & Pollock, J. (2001). *Classroom instruction that works: Research-based strategies for increasing student achievement.* Alexandria, VA: Association for Supervision and Curriculum Development.

McKee, J., & Ogle, D. (2005). *Integrating instruction: Literacy and science.* New York: Guilford Press.

McLaughlin, M., & Allen, B. (2002). *Guided comprehension: A teaching model for grades 3–8.* Newark, DE: International Reading Association.

Metsisto, D. (2005). Reading in the mathematics classroom. In J. Kenney, E. Hancewicz, L. Heuer, D. Metsisto, & C. Tuttle (Eds.), *Literacy strategies for improving mathematics instruction* (pp. 9–23). Alexandria, VA: Association for Supervision and Curriculum Development.

Moline, S. (1995). *I see what you mean: Children at work with visual information.* York, ME: Stenhouse.

Moyer, P. (2001). Using representations to explore perimeter and area. *Teaching Children Mathematics, 8*(1), 52–59.

Murray, M. (2004). *Teaching mathematics vocabulary in context.* Portsmouth, NH: Heinemann.

National Council of Teachers of English/International Reading Association. (1996). *Standards for the English language arts.* Urbana, IL: National Council of Teachers of English.

National Council of Teachers of Mathematics. (2000). *Principles and standards for school mathematics.* Reston, VA: Author.

National Reading Panel. (2002). *Teaching children to read: An evidence-based assessment of the scientific research literature on reading and its implications for reading instruction.* Bethesda, MD: National Institute of Child Health and Human Development.

O'Brien, T., & Moss, A. (2004). Real math? *Phi Delta Kappan, 86*(4), 292–296.

Oczkus, L. (2004). *Super 6 comprehension strategies: 35 lessons and more for reading success.* Norwood, MA: Christopher Gordon.

Ogle, D. (1986). KWL: A teaching model that develops active reading of expository text. *Reading Teacher, 39,* 564–570.

Ogle, D. (1992). Problem-solving and language arts instruction. In C. Collins & J. N. Mangieri (Eds.), *Teaching thinking: An agenda for the twenty-first century* (pp. 28–39). Hillsdale, NJ: Erlbaum.

Olivares, R. (1996). Communication in mathematics for students with limited English proficiency. In P. C. Elliot & M. J. Kenny (Eds.), *Communication in mathematics, K–12 and beyond* (pp. 219–230). Reston, VA: National Council of Teachers of Mathematics.

Opitz, M., & Ford, M. (2001). *Reaching readers*. Portsmouth, NH: Heinemann.

Pape, S. (2004). Middle school children's problem-solving behavior: A cognitive analysis from a reading comprehension perspective. *Journal for Research in Mathematics Education, 35*(3), 187–219.

Pressley, M. (2006). *Reading instruction that works: The case for balanced teaching* (3rd ed.). New York: Guilford Press.

Pressley, M., Allington, R., Wharton-McDonald, R., Block, C., & Morrow, L. (2001). *Learning to read lessons from exemplary first-grade classrooms*. New York: Guilford Press.

Reys, B., Reys, R., & Chavez, O. (2004). Why mathematics textbooks matter. *Educational Leadership, 61*(5), 61–66.

Rogers, A., & Rogers, E. (2004). *Scaffolding literacy instruction: Strategies for K–4 classrooms*. Portsmouth, NH: Heinemann.

Saul, M. (2006). "Radical" math becomes the standard. *Education Update, 48*, 1–2, 8.

Schwartz, R., & Raphael, T. (1985). Concept of definition: A key to improving students' vocabulary. *The Reading Teacher, 30*, 198–205.

Serafini, F. (2004). *Lessons in comprehension*. Portsmouth, NH: Heinemann.

Shadle-Talbert, D., Rahn, K., & McMahon, K. (2000). Math + literature = connections. *Illinois Reading Council Journal, 28*(2), 28–39.

Shiro, M. (1997). *Integrating children's literature and mathematics in the classroom: Children as meaning makers, problem-solvers, and literacy critics*. New York: Teachers College Press.

Smolkin, L. B., & Donovan, C. A. (2002). Oh excellent, excellent question! In C. C. Block & M. Pressley (Eds.), *Comprehension instruction: Research-based best practices* (pp. 140–157). New York: Guilford Press.

Sullivan, P. (1991). *Communication in the classroom: The importance of good questioning*. Geelong, Victoria, Australia: Deakin University Press.

Thiessen, D., Mathias, M., & Smith, J. (1998). *The wonderful world of mathematics: A critically annotated list of children's books in mathematics*. Reston, VA: National Council of Teachers of Mathematics.

Usiskin, A. (1996). Mathematics as a language. In P. C. Elliot & M. J. Kenny (Eds.), *Communication in mathematics, K–12 and beyond* (pp. 321–343). Reston, VA: National Council of Teachers of Mathematics.

Usiskin, Z. (2003). The integration of the school mathematics curriculum in the United States: History and meaning. In S. McGraw (Ed.), *Integrated mathematics: Choices and challenges* (pp. 13–32). Reston, VA: National Council of Teachers of Mathematics.

Vacca, R. T., & Vacca, J. L. (1999). *Content area reading: Literacy and learning across the curriculum* (6th ed.). Menlo Park, CA: Longman.

Van de Walle, J. (2003). *Elementary and middle school mathematics* (5th ed.). Boston: Allyn & Bacon.

Vygotsky, L. (1978). *Mind in society*. Cambridge, MA: Harvard University Press.

Weiss, I., & Pasley, J. (2004). What is high-quality instruction? *Educational Leadership, 61*(5), 24–28.

Whitin, P., & Whitin, D. (2000). *Math is language too*. Urbana, IL: National Council of Teachers of English.

Wiggins, G., & McTighe, J. (1998). *Understanding by design*. Alexandria, VA: Association for Supervision and Curriculum Development.

Wilde, S., & Whitin, D. (1992). *Read any good math lately?* Portsmouth, NH: Heinemann.

Willingham, D. T. (2002). Allocating student study time: Massed versus distributed practice. *American Educator, 26*(2), 37–39.

Young, E., & Marroquin, C. (2006). Posing problems from children's literature. *Teaching Children Mathematics, 12*(7), 362–367.

CHILDREN'S LITERATURE

Axelrod, A. (1991). *Pigs on the move*. New York: Scholastic.

Axelrod A. (1994). *Pigs will be pigs*. New York: Four Winds Press.

Burns, M. (1994). *The greedy triangle*. New York: Scholastic.

Burns, M. (1997). *Spaghetti and meatballs for all!* New York: Scholastic.

Cristaldi, K. (1996). *Even Steven and odd Todd*. New York: Scholastic.

Demi. (1997). *One grain of rice*. New York: Scholastic.

Dolan, G. (2001). *The Greenwich guide to measuring time*. Royal Observatory, Greenwich, UK: Heinemann Library.

Elliot, R. (2004). *The speedy cheetah*. Washington, DC: National Geographic Society.

Franco, B. (2001). *The little red hen in funny fairy tale math*. New York: Scholastic.

Friedman, A. (1994). *A cloak for the dreamer*. New York: Scholastic.

Griffiths R., & Clyne, M. (2004). *Games kids play*. Washington, DC: National Geographic Society.

Griffiths R., & Clyne, M. (2005). *Tim's ice cream store*. Washington, DC: National Geographic Society.

Huntingdale, R. (2004). *Giraffes*. Washington, DC: National Geographic Society.

Irons, C.(1993). *Baby bear quilt*. San Francisco: Mimosa.

Johnson, R. L. (2004). *Crunching numbers*. Washington, DC: National Geographic Society.

Kramer, A. (2003). *No math day at school*. Pelham, NY: Benchmark Education.

Lasky, K. (1994). *The librarian who measured the earth*. Boston: Little Brown Young.

McKissack, P. C. (1992). *A million fish . . . more or less*. New York: Knopf

Murphy, S. (1999). *Sand castle Saturday*. New York: HarperCollins.

Neuschwander, C. (1997). *Sir Cumference and the first round table: A math adventure*. Watertown, MA: Charlesbridge.

Neuschwander, C. (1998). *Amanda Bean's amazing dream*. New York: Scholastic.

Nguyen, J. (2006). *Comparing sizes and weights*. Washington, DC: National Geographic Society.

Novakowski, J. (2005). *A walk in the rainforest*, Vernon Hills, IL: ETA Cuisinaire.

O'Sullivan, R. (2004a). *Numbers and you*. Washington, DC: National Geographic Society.

O'Sullivan, R. (2004b). *Protecting sea turtles*. Washington, DC: National Geographic Society.

Pinczes, E. (1993). *One hundred hungry ants*. New York: Scholastic.

Pinczes, E. (1995). *A remainder of one*. New York: Scholastic.

Pollard, C. (2004). *Big bend adventure*. Washington, DC: National Geographic Society.

Pullen, R. (2004). *Which is the tallest?* Washington, DC: National Geographic Society.

Russell, S. (2004). *Animal records.* Washington, DC: National Geographic Society.

Tang, G. (2004). *Grapes of math.* New York: Scholastic.

Terban, M. (1982). *Eight ate: A feast of homonym riddles.* New York: Houghton Mifflin.

Tompert, A. (1990). *Grandfather Tang's story.* New York: Crown.

Wells, R. E. (1993). *Is a blue whale the biggest thing there is?* Morton Grove, IL: Albert Whitman.

INDEX

"f" following a page number indicates a figure; "t" following a page number indicates a table.